THOMAS WOLF

W9-DCV-951

THE NONPROFIT ORGANIZATION

An Operating Manual

Prentice-Hall, Inc., Englewood Cliffs, New Jersey 07032

Library of Congress Cataloging in Publication Data

WOLF, THOMAS, (date)
    The nonprofit organization.

    Includes index.
    1. Corporations, Nonprofit—Management.   I.   Title.
HD62.6.W65   1984   658'.048   83-19081
ISBN 0-13-623323-6
ISBN 0-13-623315-5 (pbk.)

For my parents,

Irene and Walter Wolf,

who have contributed time, money, and
children to nonprofit organizations.

This book is available at a special discount when ordered in bulk quantities. Contact Prentice-Hall, Inc., General Publishing Division, Special Sales, Englewood Cliffs, N.J. 07632.

Editorial/production supervision by Susie L. Cioffi
Cover design by Abner Graboff
Manufacturing buyer: Edward J. Ellis

ISBN 0-13-623315-5 {PBK.}
ISBN 0-13-623323-6

10 9 8 7 6 5 4

Contents

Preface

At the age of fifteen, I had my first opportunity to run a nonprofit organization. The organization was a summer music festival with an annual budget of just over $4,000. Like many nonprofit administrators, I had no experience or training in management. My training had been in music. Although this equipped me with the skills to play concerts, it did not prepare me for managing a budget, fund raising, dealing with a board of directors, planning a marketing campaign, or any of the other responsibilities that are part and parcel of nonprofit administration.

Twenty years later, as the executive director of a foundation that gave grants to nonprofit organizations, I realized that my own experience had not been unusual. Nonprofit organizations are often run by people who know almost nothing about administration but whose experience and training are rich in other areas. Most of these people seem to know a lot about the kinds of activities or services that their organizations offer, but it is probably fair to say that many of the nonprofit administrators come to their first jobs without any significant management background or training. The good ones use the job as an opportunity to learn, take courses, read books, and generally play a game of catch-up in learning how to manage. The others become frustrated, burn themselves out, and eventually leave their organizations. As a consequence, the turnover rate among administrators in nonprofit organizations is very high.

It is not only administrators of nonprofit organizations who are largely unschooled. Consider the committed volunteers who, after years of service to a hospital (or a museum or a community center), are asked to join the board. Like many of the individuals who accept positions on boards, these people do so without any conception of the responsibilities of trusteeship. This is a serious problem for nonprofit organizations. When the governing group does not know how to govern, when roles and responsibilities are not clear, the organization's ability to carry out its mission is compromised.

v

This book is a primer for people in nonprofit organizations who wish to increase their understanding of those organizations and hone various administrative skills. It is also for students who wish to learn about management issues in the nonprofit world. It is based on material developed for a seminar on the administration of nonprofit organizations at Radcliffe College, a seminar open to graduate students and working professionals. As a result, this book is neither exclusively theoretical nor solely practical. Theory and practice are both discussed so that the reader can gain an understanding of the *context* in which decisions are made and learn the reasons why certain kinds of techniques seem to work.

The various chapters of this book introduce readers to some of the more important areas of nonprofit administration. Not one of the chapters represents a complete and definitive treatment of the subject matter. Indeed, whole books have been written on each of the topics covered, and I urge you to follow up with additional reading in areas that pique your interest and curiosity. Practically speaking, though, many readers will probably not have time to search out and read those longer works. This book provides the broad overview that is so often lacking among board members and managers. Such an overview is essential. For, in the end, no nonprofit organization can continue to flourish unless it is governed and managed responsibly.

Acknowledgments

This book is based on material developed for a seminar I have taught for several years at Radcliffe College. I would like to thank my students who provided many of the best ideas for the book. I am also grateful to Nancy Downey, Director of the Radcliffe Seminars, who originally encouraged me to develop the course material.

I would like to thank Mary Van Someren Cok, Pat Doran, and Henry Bromelkamp for their help on Chapter 7. Ms. Cok also provided many of the examples for Chapter 6. Roger Neugebauer assisted with the section on cash flow in Chapter 5. A special thanks to Mary Kennan and Suse Cioffi of the General Publishing Division of Prentice-Hall.

Finally, I am especially grateful to Ann Backus, who read the entire manuscript and made substantial editorial suggestions.

1

The World of Nonprofit Organizations

Suppose you asked someone the question: "What is an elephant?" and the person answered: "An elephant is not a horse." You would probably find the answer unsatisfactory. Yet, when people talk about nonprofit organizations they generally describe them in a similar way.

Indeed, the very term *nonprofit organization* says very little about the creature it is meant to describe. It says only what the creature is *not*—it is not a profit-making entity. But it says nothing about what it is.

This observation is significant. It is not easy to describe what nonprofit organizations are, or should be, and this makes managing them a difficult job frought with challenges and problems. Unlike management issues in the profit sector, which tend to be clear and related to specific economic measures, issues in the nonprofit environment are more nebulous because they relate to the more abstract concept of "public service." In a profit-making company, a manager generally knows whether he or she is doing a good job, but it is often less clear in a nonprofit organization in which the primary purpose is not to make money but to serve the public.

Yet, the fact that nonprofit organizations have public service missions can easily be misconstrued. It might suggest that privately incorporated nonprofits are simply "private sector" versions of public (governmental) agencies, organized to solve some societal problem or deliver some much needed or desired service. But nonprofit organizations are not the same as public agencies. For one thing, although private nonprofit organizations have a public service mission, they do not necessarily have a stated or implied mandate of "equity" (that is, a mandate to serve everyone) the way public agencies usually do. As a result, the nonprofit organization's actual constituency may be far more limited than that of a public agency working in the same field. An additional difference concerns the entrepreneurial nature of nonprofits: Many engage in all sorts of money-making ventures that cause a closer resemblance to profit-making entities than to public agencies.

In fact, a nonprofit organization is neither in the profit sector nor in the public sector but sits somewhere between the two. This position allows the nonprofit great flexibility in its operation but also requires great skill in its management. On the one hand, managers must learn the same management techniques and analytical strategies that apply in the profit sector. However, while it is true that many of these techniques are relevant in the nonprofit world, their application is dissimilar. Indeed, although both profit-making and nonprofit organizations engage in planning, budgeting, accounting, and marketing, although both have to contend with issues of governance, personnel, and information management, and although both have to raise money from time to time, these activities are carried out in markedly different ways. Similarly, while it may be useful to know about the workings of a public agency and the development of public policy, it is not sufficient preparation for the nonprofit manager or trustee. These individuals must come to understand the special characteristics of nonprofit organizations.

WHAT IS A NONPROFIT ORGANIZATION?

In this book, the term *nonprofit organization* refers to those legally constituted, nongovernmental entities, incorporated under state law as charitable or not-for-profit corporations that have been set up to serve some public purpose and are tax exempt according to the United States Internal Revenue Service. All must have the following four characteristics.

1. They must be incorporated and they must have a public purpose.
2. Their governance structured must preclude self-interest and private financial gain.
3. They must be exempt from paying federal tax.
4. They must possess the special legal status that stipulates gifts made to them are tax deductible.

Consequently, nonprofit organizations as described in this book do not include entities that have been set up to make a profit but are failing to do so; nor do they include those organizations that are governed informally by a collection of people who, although they have banded together to serve some public good, have been granted no special corporate status by federal and state authorities. Such organizations do not have all the characteristics previously listed, and consequently their missions, governance, and method of management are significantly different from the organizations that are described in this book.

This chapter considers four major challenges that face nonprofit organizations as a consequence of these special characteristics. The challenges include:

1. Articulating a clear public service mission.
2. Testing for organized abandonment.
3. Engaging in risk/survival analysis.
4. Identifying and involving the constituency.

CONSEQUENCES OF A PUBLIC SERVICE MISSION

The difference between profit and nonprofit organizations centers around the concept of mission. The ultimate mission of the profit-making entity is to earn money for its "owners." Ownership can come in many forms, of course, from outright ownership of the organization by a single individual to shared ownership (by partners or shareholders or some other group). This concept of ownership is completely absent from nonprofit organizations and consequently the nonprofit's mission has a totally different thrust. There can be no owners in a nonprofit organization because such an entity is intended to serve a broad public purpose and the law is clear in specifying that ownership (with concommitant private gain) is incompatible with public purpose. This is not to say that nonprofit organizations cannot make money. Nonprofit organizations can and do make money—in the same way profit-making entities do—but the money that is taken in must be directed toward the public purpose for which the organization was set up or, if this is impossible, held in reserve or turned over to another organization with a public purpose.

It is much more difficult to identify and articulate the mission of a nonprofit organization and consequently to develop criteria by which success can be measured. In a profit-making organization, because the mission is clear, success criteria are also clear. Because the mission centers on profitability, the criteria for success (and for decision making) include variables like the bottom line, return on investment, sales, profit margins, market share, and other easily calculated measures. In the nonprofit organization where the mission centers around public service, it is not only more difficult to define purposes, but it can be a bewildering task to try to find the proper yardstick by which to measure success. If the purpose of a school is to produce well-educated citizens, if an arts organization is set up to offer high quality theatrical events, if a hospital is supposed to deliver top-flight health care, what criteria should each use to measure success? There will always be quantitative measures at hand: college board scores for the school, audience size for the theatre, numbers of patients for the hospital, but these measures are only indirect indices of success. More closely related indications, at least easily measurable ones, generally are harder to find.

Because the missions of nonprofit organizations center on the concept of public service, one might look to the public sector for models that demonstrate how mission statements are articulated and tested. Unfortunately, there is a problem with this approach. In the public sector, there is an implied or stated mandate of "equity" in every mission statement. That is, public agencies are obligated to serve anyone who is eligible for assistance. For that reason, quantitative measures of success are often possible on the basis of the numbers of people served, their geographic distribution, their racial and socioeconomic diversity, and the cost-effectiveness of service delivery. For nonprofit organizations, these criteria may be relevant, but more often than not they are only indirect measures of success. Consider a nonprofit university-affiliated teaching hospital. Unlike the public hospital down the street, it cannot directly measure its success by counting the numbers of patients served and the cost-effectiveness of medical treatment. The nonprofit hospital's mission of promoting excellence in medical practice through exemplary training is less concrete and success criteria are more difficult to establish.

Thus, we come to the first major challenge for a nonprofit organization—the challenge of *articulating a clear public service mission*. The challenge is not only to come up with a statement that defines what the organization is and what it has been set up to do but to state these things in such a way that the organization can evaluate its success in carrying out this mission over time.

THE TEST FOR ORGANIZED ABANDONMENT

If one of the greatest challenges for a nonprofit organization is to determine whether or not it is fulfilling its mission, it is equally difficult to decide at what point the organization is no longer needed or wanted. A so-called *test for organized abandonment* is so difficult to apply that many nonprofit organizations simply struggle along year after year without ever facing up to the fact that their existence is of very little consequence to anyone outside of the organization itself.

Consider the organization whose mission centers on the eradication of a particular disease. What should happen to that organization when a cure for the disease is discovered, medicine made available, and the disease eliminated? At first glance, it would seem obvious that the organization should disband. But should it? It has over the years built up a loyal constituency. Might that constituency be encouraged to join the fight to eliminate another disease?

Or consider the organization that has been allowed to atrophy over the years and now finds itself surrounded by a number of younger, more vital organizations that appear to be carrying out its mission more effectively? This would appear to be a clear case where the organization should disband. But again, one should not jump quickly to conclusions. By whose standards is the organization judged moribund and by what criteria is it determined that others are carrying out its mission more effectively?

The concept of organized abandonment is central to our understanding of nonprofit organizations and illustrates one of the principal difficulties in responsible governance and management. "Organized abandonment" refers to the planned phasing out of an organization's operation. The word "organized" is used to characterize a kind of disbanding that is the result of careful deliberation rather than of unwelcome and unexpected financial reversals, management upheaval, or other external or internal crises. One of the major problems in the nonprofit world is that the test for organized abandonment is difficult to apply because the criteria by which judgements are made are relative and subjective.

Once again, the contrast with the profit and public sectors is clear. In the profit sector, when an organization loses money for any length of time and the future does not promise a turn-around, it is usually a signal that something *must* change. Investors move in to cut their losses and the organization may be sold, disbanded, or reorganized. There are two essential differences in the nonprofit sector. The first is that it is not nearly as obvious *when* things should change because there is not a single, objective criterion by which to measure success or failure. Second, there is not the predictable outside pressure to reorganize or disband. Because there is no voting group moving quickly to protect its investments, the governing group and staff can continue operating for years without a real sense of purpose or standard of excellence.

In the public sector, there is also a clear difference. For a governmental agency, publicly elected individuals hold the purse strings and review the agency's achievements and plans, usually on an annual basis. The agency must perform to the elected individuals' satisfaction or its funding, and sometimes its continued existence, is threatened. Periodically, the agency may be further subjected to some form of "sunset review" that requires a formal justification of its continued existence before it is "authorized" to continue operating. No such external pressures are brought to bear on private nonprofit organizations.

We have arrived, then, at what might be called the second major challenge for a nonprofit organization—the challenge of *testing for organized abandonment*. This challenge requires that the organization:

1. Has defined its mission clearly.
2. Has established success criteria by which it can evaluate the relevance and effectiveness of its mission.
3. Has set up a formal system by which it can determine whether the mission is still relevant and whether it is carrying out the mission effectively.

The following case may provide insight into how this can be accomplished.

THE REGIONAL EXCHANGE

In the late 1960s, two federal agencies (in partnership with state agencies from northern New England) funded the formation of a new organization that would encourage exemplary educational and artistic programming in rural Maine, New Hampshire, and Vermont. The organization was set up as a private nonprofit corporation. Its mission was twofold: first, to improve the quality and quantity of artistic and educational offerings in the three states through workshops, performances, seminars, classes, and other kinds of events; and second, to upgrade the expertise of schools and community groups within the three states in sponsoring such offerings in order to establish permanent ongoing programs at the local level.

For ten years, the Regional Exchange thrived. Its budget increased, its staff grew to ten people, it was given a home within a large university, and its program was cited as a national model. By the late 1970s, things had begun to change: The funding of the Regional Exchange became more precarious because the federal agencies had changed their funding priorities. The funding crisis was the result of a policy shift for which the Regional Exchange was not to blame and over which it had no control. The federal funding agencies began a new initiative to set up regional centers and the Regional Exchange, because it only served three states, was not considered an appropriate recipient of the federal designation of "regional." Hence, through a technicality in federal policy, funding appeared to be uncertain.

But money was not the Regional Exchange's only problem. In 1970, the Regional Exchange's constituency had been composed largely of volunteers with little experience in educational and artistic programming. Teachers, parents, and other volunteers continually praised the technical assistance provided by the Regional Exchange staff stating that "we never could have done these programs without you." But ten years later, the Regional Exchange's constituency was becoming far more sophisticated. Many of the local programs were staffed by professionals and these people were demanding either that the organization provide better and more extensive services and programs or simply turn the federal and state money directly over to them.

It is fortunate that this organization had defined its mission clearly, set up evaluation criteria, and was willing to engage in the test for organized abandonment. By doing so, it was able to provide improved services to its constituents, preserve all of its important programs, find challenging jobs for its staff members, and, ultimately, to disband.

The organization went through the following steps to determine whether organized abandonment was necessary. An evaluation was done to determine how well the organization had fulfilled or was fulfilling its mission. Through the evaluation, it was discovered that the ten years of developmental work in rural northern New England had spawned a large number of ongoing, self-sufficient programs in both the schools and community organizations—a discovery that pleased the board but indicated that the need for developmental work had diminished. The evaluation also revealed that while the need for educational and arts resources was still great, the Regional Exchange's constituents were looking to the larger and better funded organizations to provide these resources, and that the Regional Exchange was becoming less important to them.

Subsequent to the evaluation, the board and staff of the Regional Exchange talked to funders in both the public and private sectors to analyze the financial prospects for the future. While most of the funders said that they would be willing to help the Regional Exchange by making small gifts toward the organization's programs, no funder was willing to underwrite the basic administrative costs of the organization. Because the federal agency that had originally provided the administrative underwriting was in the process of designating another organization (which serviced six states) to be the "official" regional organization, and because federal policy required that only one organization per region could receive the basic administrative underwriting, the Regional Exchange's financial future did not look good.

The board and the staff of the Regional Exchange met for several months to consider the situation. Should the organization change its mission in order to secure basic administrative funding? Should the organization charge for its services? Should the staff be cut to one or two people so that the organization could continue to run a token program, hoping for a better future later? Each of these alternatives and many others were considered. But each was rejected. The original mission of the organization had been right for its time. Much of what the organization had set out to do, it had accomplished. Now there were other organizations that were carrying out the balance of the mission with greater effectiveness and financial viability.

The board voted to disband, but set up a nine-month timetable to make sure that every significant program of the Regional Exchange was placed in another organization, that each member of the staff had another place to go, and that a history of the organization and its accomplishments could be written to become a part of the public record. Several of the programs were absorbed by the new six-state regional organization, based in Massachusetts; and, to assure continuity through the first year of transition, that organization hired the Regional Exchange's Executive Director as a full-time consultant/coordinator for program implementation in the three northern New England states. In June of 1980, the Regional Exchange closed its doors. It did so after a champagne reception to celebrate its accomplishments and the future of its programs.

The history of the Regional Exchange is a success story in nonprofit administration. Its success is represented not only by what it accomplished during its scant eleven years of existence, but also what it accomplished in disbanding at the right time and in the right way. There are many nonprofit organizations that would benefit from a close analysis of the history of the Regional Exchange, particularly the events of the final two years. This history demonstrates how a nonprofit organization can meet the challenge of mission accountability.

INSTITUTIONAL SURVIVAL VERSUS PUBLIC SERVICE

"For several years we've had a serious cash flow problem," said Mr. X, "and until that's solved we won't be originating any new programs. Balancing the books has become our top priority."

This statement was made by the chairperson of the board of a prominent nonprofit organization in Texas. His "safety first" attitude suggests that he may have forgotten the organization's original mission or has relegated it to a second-level priority. He seems to be telling us that running a nonprofit organization is just like running a business, that financial problems have to be tended to first. In some ways he may be right. After all, no organization, profit or nonprofit, can lose money forever and survive. But perhaps it is not quite that simple. There may be many ways to meet a financial crisis, some more consistent with the organization's mission than others. As one observer put it: "Given the present crisis, it is clear that cuts will have to be made; it's the nature of the cuts that has people concerned."

Here is a classic manifestation of one of the great dilemmas for nonprofit organizations. Which is more important? To assure the continuity and the survival of the organization? Or to stay true to the organization's mission even if this involves certain financial and institutional risks? Consider the following cases.

1. A legal aid group must decide whether it will begin to charge clients a modest fee in order to generate much needed earned income (the mission statement talks about providing free legal aid).
2. A church must decide whether to take a stand on abortion. Regardless of the position it takes, it risks alienating a large number of church members. Yet the minister believes that the mission of the church is to provide guidance on moral issues.

3. An all-male school, responding to decreasing enrollments, has been advised by a marketing consultant to "go co-ed." Yet the faculty and many alumni feel that the original mission to offer a quality education to young men, is still valid.

4. A symphony orchestra, organized to improve the quality of the musical life of its city, must decide whether to increase the number of "pops" concerts and decrease its regular subscription concerts of classical music. The programming change would assist the organization in meeting its payroll but would compromise the mission of the organization.

5. A women's health organization, founded as a "collective," must decide whether it will reorganize around more conventional management lines in order to increase efficiency and professionalism. Several of the organization's founders believe that "collective" management is central to the organization's mission.

Each of these examples suggests a choice between risks and compromises. The original missions of the various organizations suggest one direction; prudence and good management sense suggest another. Staying true to the original missions may be risky and expensive, yet focussing only on the relative security of organizational survival may lead to a compromise in principles. The tug between these two competing tendencies is constant in the nonprofit environment, and it becomes extreme when organizations are under pressure, when funds are scarce, and when there is lack of agreement about basic purposes.

Once again, the contrast with the public and profit sectors is striking. In the public sector, risk is measured in political terms and agencies generally have a clear idea of how far they can and should go. The authorization to operate comes from elected officials who set limits on what is permissible. To extend these limits requires political persuasion, advocacy, and, in extreme cases, a change brought about by voters who put new people in office. In the profit sector, businesses are constantly faced with choices involving varying degrees of risk. But the risks are always measured in terms of the ultimate return or payoff. If the effect of a risky decision today is greater profitability tomorrow, then the decision may have merit. If greater profitability is unlikely, there is no reason to take the risk. Once again, the decision criterion is clear because the organization's mission is clear. Profit-making organizations will rarely look for ways to serve the public that involve increased risks and costs without any possibility of increased profits.

The situation for the nonprofit organization is different because the standards of value are not stated primarily in financial terms. Who can decide how much it is worth to take a political stand, perform more classical music, preserve a "collective" decision-making structure, or continue to provide free legal aid? Risk in each case does not lead to greater profitability. In fact, in most cases, risk places greater financial burdens on the organization. Thus, there is no single simple criterion on which to base a decision. It is a judgement call. In one camp, some say the organization cannot afford to put itself in jeopardy; in the other camp, people claim that a nonprofit organization that does not stay true to its ideals should not continue to operate.

The lesson to be learned is that there is rarely a "correct" place to draw the line between organizational security and a public service mission. A nonprofit organization, which is responsibly governed and managed, finds itself debating the question continually, issue by issue, decision by decision. Thus, we come to the third major challenge for a nonprofit organization—*risk/survival analysis*, or the search for the proper balance between organization extension and risk taking and organizational security. This challenge involves:

1. The existence of an ongoing planning process.
2. An ability to analyze future options from both a practical and an idealistic point of view.
3. A willingness to debate the pros and cons of each proposed action in terms of the organization's stated mission and its long-term security.

Consider the following example of an organization that successfully met this challenge.

LEGAL EDUCATION SOCIETY

The Legal Education Society has been in existence for several decades. Its mission is to provide legal assistance in a variety of ways—legal aid to individuals who cannot afford it; legal assistance to nonprofit organizations; and scholarly contributions to advance the public's understanding of the law. The multi-racial board of directors of the Legal Education Society is composed of lawyers, judges, and private citizens representing different socio-economic groups. Today, the organization is adequately funded, has a modest endowment, and has a permanent staff of 12 people.

In 1976, the Legal Education Society hired as its executive director a woman who was widely recognized as one of the brightest young lawyers in the country. She had been on the Law Review at a prestigious law school, had contributed significantly to the law literature, and had spent two years clerking for a Supreme Court justice. Her appointment was hailed as a turning point in the history of the Legal Education Society. However, it was a turning point in a way that no one expected.

During the first four years of her tenure as executive director, the young woman pleased everyone. She added programs, secured increased funding, wrote important articles, attracted new staff (including minorities and women), and appeared to be the dynamo that everyone thought she would be when they hired her. After four years, her interest began to shift. With her growing prominence in the field, organizations throughout the country wanted to hire her as a consultant to advise them on setting up legal education programs. At first, she accepted these assignments only on weekends or vacations, having received permission to do so from the board of directors. But as the demand for her consulting services grew, as her own interest in these projects increased, and as the scope of the projects demanded greater time commitments, she asked the board whether she might set up a small consulting program through the Legal Education Society, bringing the consulting contracts through the organization. The advantage, she explained, would be that the Legal Education Society could earn income and expand its influence nationally in the field of legal education.

At first, the arrangement worked well. Two large contracts during the first year brought in $42,000 of additional income. The Legal Education Society was cited in the literature as a leader in its field. The executive director, now with assistance of several key staff people, continued to be happy with the challenge and growth of the consulting work, but the Legal Education Society's primary constituency back home was becoming restless. The focus of the organization was changing. Individual staff members appeared to be less interested in their constituents' problems as the members became more focussed on the problems facing people half way across the country. The board of directors was receiving conflicting signals. The national press (and funding agencies throughout the country) were praising the work of the Legal Education Society; the local constituency (individuals and organizations seeking legal assistance) were complaining about inadequate service.

On the fifth anniversary of the executive director's tenure, she proposed a major restructuring of the Legal Education Society in which the consulting business would become—within five years—the major activity of the organization. Her plan, brilliant in its conception, saw the organization doubling in budget and staff during that period and becoming far less reliant on unearned income. Legal assistance would still be provided, but it would be offered through a number of subcontracts and the Legal Education Society would simply act as broker. One of her justifications for the plan was especially compelling. At the time, federal and state governments seemed to be placing less priority on the funding of legal aid programs, and the private sector did not indicate enthusiasm about making up the difference. Realistically, there was less money available and greater competition for that money. By way of contrast, the consulting business offered a very promising financial future.

There was no question in the minds of those serving on the board of directors that the executive director could pull off the plan. Her ability had been proven time and time again. There was also no debate on the question of the short-term funding outlook. Simply stated, the funding picture for basic legal services looked bleak. However, the board of directors was concerned about what impact the change would have on the organization's central and original mission. Although a consulting business would assure organizational survival and continued growth, it would also mean a major shift away from basic legal services for the poor and for nonprofit organizations. That need existed, now more than ever, and several community members of the board of directors argued passionately that the organization must return to its original purpose.

The question was debated for two months. Surveys were conducted both among constituents and national authorities. In the end, the board of directors, in a close vote, turned down the executive director's request and called for a new plan that would return the organization to its original mission. A year later, the Legal Education Society had a new executive director, a smaller (and mostly new) staff, a smaller budget, many new board members, and a clear sense of its place in the community. The executive director had started her own consulting firm, which was staffed with many of her former employees. One of her first clients turned out to be the Legal Education Society, which even today continues to draw on her experience and expertise.

Did the board of directors make the right decision? Some people would say "yes," some would say "no." In the end, there was no right decision because "right" depended on each person's point of view. In spite of this, there was a correct and responsible course of action, and it was the one the board of directors chose when they decided to debate the executive director's plan in an open and informed manner. They considered the question of mission on the one hand and organizational security on the other. They weighed their options and came down in favor of a recommitment to the original mission. Those who disagreed (the executive director, some staff, some board members), left the organization, and although they were unhappy with the decision, all believed in the integrity of the decision-making process. The organization had successfully met the challenge of risk/survival analysis.

HOW LARGE AND DIVERSE A "PUBLIC"?

The mission of every nonprofit organization centers on serving the public. But what precisely does that mean? The public, in the broadest sense, is everyone; yet few nonprofit organizations see themselves as offering their services to "everyone." Unlike public agencies, they do not operate under any such implied or stated obligation. Therefore, every nonprofit organization must decide how broadly to define its constituency and how large or diverse a public to serve.

This decision is not simply a theoretical one. It is practical. The decision has ramifications for programs and activities, for budget, for staff size and structure. It touches on questions of appropriate constituency representation on the board. It is a question that cannot be finessed through a mission statement that refers in a general sort of way to the fact that the organization "serves the public." The organization must demonstrate the scope of its service and interests through its governance, its staffing, and through its programs and activities.

The contrast with profit-sector organizations sharpens our understanding of this special characteristic of nonprofits. In the profit sector, an organization's public is determined by its need to sell products and services. Therefore, its public consists of those who have either a direct or indirect effect on profitability: its customers and clients, its employees, and those significant others who can either promote or hamper the organization's ability to carry out its activities. In the case of a beer manufacturer, this latter group might include a senator considering "bottle bill" legislation; for a major armaments manufacturer it might include an anti-war protester who is also a newspaper writer.

Each of these constituency groups—customers/clients, employees, and significant others—are important to a profit-making entity to the extent that they can influence the business enterprise. The primary strategy for dealing with each group is determined solely from a business point of view. For example, it may turn out that it is more practical and profitable to deal with these groups at arm's length rather than involve them in the decision-making structure. Thus, a business may survey the attitudes and predilections of its customers and clients, adjust its products and services accordingly, and then adopt marketing strategies to promote an image of "service." It might offer its employees a generous "benefits" package or a bonus to promote good management/employee relations. In some cases, it might decide to make certain kinds of "investments" to promote a positive public image among those whose opinions can affect the conduct of business and, ultimately, profitability. For example, the business may make contributions to political candidates to try to "influence" legislation or it may make charitable contributions to "promote" an image of a "caring" organization. When these decisions are justified to the organization's "owners" or "investors," they are justified on the basis that they promote the business' own interests. In all cases, service to and involvement of various constituency groups is seen as a strategy, and in no case is involvement of the constituency in the decision-making process seen as essential.

In the nonprofit world, the situation is completely reversed. Service to the public is not seen as a strategy; it is an end in itself. While a nonprofit organization can engage in many of the same activities that were described for the profit-making business—surveying its constituency to adjust products/services, promoting harmony among employees, even, occasionally, making contributions to political campaigns or to charities—it does so out of a conviction that these activities further the organization's service mission. In order to be effective, the organization will have to do more than keep its public at arm's length. Broad involvement of its public at all levels of operation is absolutely necessary to achieve effective nonprofit administration.

Yet, the nonprofit organization does not have the same kind of public mandate that the governmental (or public) agency does. The public agency, because it is tax based in its support, theoretically must offer its services to anyone. In many cases, "anyone" is restricted to people or organizations meeting certain eligibility requirements. But there are two significant points here. First, eligibility is always defined precisely, usually in *quantitative* terms (for example, people over 65, people who earn less than $6,000/year, organizations with budgets of less than $100,000/year, nonprofit 501(c)(3) organizations). Second, once eligibility criteria are set, *anyone* who meets those criteria can expect to be served. Not so with the nonprofit organization. Such an organization has the luxury of picking and choosing who it wishes to serve. But this very flexibility is also a challenge. Defining the constituency too narrowly or failing to include representatives of that constituency in the operation of a nonprofit organization may have negative consequences.

Indeed, this is the fourth major challenge for a nonprofit organization, the challenge of *constituency identification and involvement*. A nonprofit organization must identify clearly those it intends to serve, and once it does so it must work toward an organizational structure—through board, staff, and activities—which reinforces its commitment to that group. The various decisions that follow the identification of an organization's constituents establish its specific image in the community, provide a clue to potential funders concerning its public commitment, and either attract or repel the very people the organization wishes to serve.

Why is this issue so important? Consider the following situations.

1. An art museum fails to secure a grant from its state arts agency because its programs "serve only an elitist and affluent audience." It is encouraged to find ways to "reach out" to a broader public.

2. A health clinic based in an urban ghetto claims to be serving its community that is composed of 80% black residents. Yet, despite efforts to attract blacks to the clinic, nearly all of the clinic's patients are white. Significantly, so are its entire board and staff.
3. The board of directors of a community recreation center is mystified by the low attendance at a newly planned series of events. The problem stems from the fact that the events were planned by a consultant who failed to seek community input.
4. The Internal Revenue Service challenges the tax-exempt status of a nonprofit literary marketing service on the grounds that membership is open only to a select few who derive clear financial benefits from the association.

Each of these organizations finds itself in a dilemma. In each case, the concept of public involvement has been construed too narrowly.

- In the first case, that of the art museum, the program director of the funding agency that dispenses public tax dollars says her grants committee is unwilling to "see the taxes of poor people going to pay for the pleasures of the rich" (those who participate in the museum's activities). She claims that her agency might feel very differently if the museum offered subsidized admissions for senior citizens, attempted to make the facility accessible to the handicapped, provided informal concerts in community locations, or offered an educational program for local school children.
- In the case of the health center, the organization's mission statement speaks about service to the community; but the organization's all white board and staff transmit a different message to the black people in that community. It is a case where actions speak louder than words.
- In the case of the recreation center, the organization appears to have alienated its primary community constituency by placing too much confidence in the abilities of a consultant. Perhaps, if community representatives had been involved in the planning process from the start, there would have been a greater sense of ownership once the programs were established.
- Finally, the literary organization offers a chilling preview of what can happen when an organization defines its membership and services too narrowly. The consequences of ambiguity about the nonprofit intent of the organization are possible loss of funding and ultimately of tax-exempt status as well.

Meeting the challenge of public service involves the following components.

1. A clear statement of purpose.
2. A well-defined understanding of an organization's constituency.
3. Involvement of this constituency at all levels of the organization, but particularly at the trustee level.

4. Programs and activities that demonstrate a strong commitment to the constituency.

SUMMARY

The purpose of this chapter is to describe some of the more important characteristics of nonprofit organizations and the consequent challenges that face those that govern and manage them. Nonprofit organizations are private sector organizations with public purposes. This combination gives them great flexibility in their operation. However, flexibility is a double-edged sword. It offers opportunities yet poses certain dangers. Most particularly, it can cause ambiguity and uncertainty in the areas of mission, constituency, and activities. A nonprofit organization must address these dangers by:

— articulating its mission clearly.
— identifying its constituency and involving representatives of that constituency in all phases of the organization's operation.
— engaging in ongoing planning with an eye toward careful consideration of the risks and benefits of every proposed course of action.
— testing for "organized abandonment" in order to ensure that the organization remains needed and wanted.

These challenges, when properly met, provide a basic framework for responsible governance and management in nonprofit organizations.

2
The Board

Mary Clarke founded the Compton Community Center eleven years ago. Had she known then what she knows now, she would have done things differently. Who could have imagined back then, when the center was just an idea in her head, that the idea would become a reality, that within ten years the community center would be serving over 15,000 people a year, would own a building (a former school house that was purchased from the town for $1), have a paid staff of 22 people, and have a budget in excess of $1 million? Had she known all these things were possible, she might have taken the advice of people who told her to go more slowly and carefully. But, at the time, she felt she had to move quickly and decisively. She had to garner support from anyone who would help. She had to show confidence even when she was not sure she was doing the right thing. Her philosophy was that enthusiasm is contagious, and it is enthusiasm that builds community organizations.

Mary Clarke's biggest regret is that she did not exercise greater care in assembling a board of trustees. Her mistake is completely understandable given the circumstances. The community center had operated for two years as a project of the local YMCA and had not needed to incorporate. It was a convenient relationship. The YMCA provided space, took care of all of the necessary bookkeeping, and lent its tax-exempt status to the center so that Mary could go out and fund raise. Eventually, she knew, she would have to worry about separate corporate status but many people advised her to wait until the program was well established. However, something unexpected happened that required a change in her timetable. When Compton's School Board decided to close one of the local elementary schools, several influential people in town felt that it should become the new home for the Compton Community Center. The idea was the fulfillment of Mary Clarke's dream and she was not about to claim that the organization was not ready for such a step.

After that, things moved quickly. There was a special town referendum in which the voters agreed that the school should be sold to the Compton Community Center for $1. Lawyers for the town met with lawyers representing the YMCA and Mary Clarke's committee. All agreed that under these new circumstances Mary Clarke's "project" had gone beyond the point at which the YMCA could assume a fiscal agent status and that separate incorporation for the Compton Community Center would be a necessity. It was further agreed that Mary needed an official nonprofit corporation to which the property could be deeded.

It was at this point that Mary Clarke made her first serious mistake. In her haste to get the corporation together, she asked a group of her friends to serve as the trustees. "It is just to satisfy the lawyers," she said, "and to put some names on the incorporation papers. I promise that you won't really have to do anything." These were words that she soon came to regret. She regretted them when the Compton Community Center needed to begin serious fund raising, when she needed to mobilize support in the community for a zoning change, and when she came to realize that one person could not single-handedly assume responsibility for an organization as large and complex as the Compton Community Center was becoming. Like many nonprofit organizations, Mary's was incorporated in haste and a governing group was thrown together that knew nothing about the considerable responsibilities of trusteeship. This was to haunt Mary Clarke for the next five years.

Perhaps all of this would have been clearer if Mary Clarke herself had understood the specific role that the law has carved out for trustees[1] in connection with the governance of a legally constituted nonprofit organization. Chapter 1 indicated that a nonprofit organization is one that is granted several very lucrative concessions and immunities by the federal and state governments, especially after it has received permission to operate as a tax-exempt organization. Once the organization is declared tax exempt, government taxing authorities have given up their right to tax and, further, have agreed to allow individuals and institutions to claim tax deductions when they make gifts to the organization. This is no less than a generous public subsidy. In making this concession, the government is assuming that the organization is somehow serving the public and not operating for anyone's private financial gain.

By giving up the power to tax, the government is making a tremendous concession and indirectly giving the organization a great deal of financial assistance. For this reason, there needs to be some protection built into the system so that the government can feel that the public purpose of the organization is in fact being carried out. As a result, it requires that a group of people act as guardians of the "public trust"—individuals who have the public's interest at heart. These people are the trustees. It is their task to act as stewards, accountable to the state government that granted the organization its charter, accountable to the federal government that granted tax-exempt status, and ultimately accountable to the public itself. In order to ensure that this group of people does have the public's interest at heart, the individuals should not serve in order to derive financial benefits from trusteeship, as would be the case in a profit-making organization. Rather, they are expected to serve for the public good and to exercise, on behalf of the public, a legal and fiduciary responsibility. They must make sure both that the organization

---

[1] The word *trustee* is used here to describe a person serving on the board of trustees. Sometimes this group is referred to as the board of directors in which case those who serve are called *directors*. However, those directors who serve on the board are not to be confused with a staff person with the same title such as an executive director, a program director, or an artistic director. In general, directors who are board members do not serve on the staff and are not paid.

is carrying out its mission as articulated in the "Articles of Organization" (incorporation papers) and that its financial activities are both legal and proper given federal and state requirements.

In this context, trusteeship is a serious business. It is not simply an honor. Nor is it simply attendance at luncheons and tea parties. It is an activity that requires knowledge, commitment, and time. In selecting trustees, Mary Clarke should have found people who understood this, she should have searched out people with proper legal and financial skills. Most important, she should have looked for people who understood something about the responsibilities and duties of trusteeship.

THE RESPONSIBILITIES AND DUTIES OF TRUSTEES

There are six major areas of responsibility for trustees. Trustees should:

1. Determine the organization's mission and set policies for its operation to establish its general course from year to year.
2. Establish fiscal policy and boundaries, including budgets and financial controls.
3. Provide adequate resources for the activities of the organization through direct financial contributions and a commitment to fund raising.
4. Select, evaluate, and, if necessary, terminate the appointment of the chief executive.
5. Develop and maintain a communication link to the community.
6. Ensure that the provisions of the organization's charter and the law are being followed.

Important as it is to understand what the duties of trustees include, it is equally important to understand what they do not include. Trustees should not:

- Engage in the day-to-day operation of the organization.
- Hire staff other than the chief executive.
- Make detailed programmatic decisions more appropriately left to staff.

Let us look in more detail at the six responsibility areas of trustees.

POLICY MAKING

By law, the board of trustees is responsible for drafting (and amending when necessary) two documents that set out various rules, regulations, and procedures. These are the *Articles of Organization* and the *Bylaws*.

In addition, the trustees may wish to develop two additional documents, the *Personnel Manual* and a *Trustee Manual* to further clarify roles, responsibilities, duties, and general policies.

The *Articles of Organization*, which are initially drafted at the time of incorporation, are filed in the state office that maintains corporate records. The portion of the "articles" that sets out the basic operating framework of the organization is almost always drafted with the assistance of an attorney to ensure conformity with the law governing nonprofit corporations. The portion containing the mission statement should be drafted by the trustees. Because so much of the organization's character, structure, and reason for being are contained in the *Articles of Organization*, the trustees should review it at least once every three years. Changes should be stated as amendments, approved by the trustees, and subsequently filed with the state.

The board of trustees is also responsible for drafting a second document, called the *Bylaws*, which serves as the organization's operating constitution. Bylaws go beyond the general material contained in the "articles" and discuss more detailed and specific procedures affecting the trustees themselves. For example, the bylaws set out the number, tenure, and election procedure for trustees, discuss how and when meetings are called, how officers (president, treasurer, clerk, and so on) are elected and what their powers are, how votes are taken, how board vacancies are filled, and a host of other small details essential to the smooth operation of the organization.

Bylaws, like *Articles of Organization*, must be reviewed periodically and updated. Further, it is the responsibility of the trustees to see that the provisions are followed in order to avoid legal complications. Consider the following case.

The executive director of a nonprofit organization had been warned several times by the president of the board that the trustees were unhappy with his performance. After six months, the president held a special meeting of the executive committee, and a vote was taken to terminate the executive director. The executive director was informed of the decision and, unbeknownst to the trustees, secured the services of a lawyer. Meanwhile, a search committee was formed and a new executive director was hired. When the time came for the first executive director to leave, he stated that he had not been legally removed from his job and was therefore still the executive director. He pointed out that according to the bylaws, the executive committee was not empowered to terminate him, and that such an action required a majority vote of the entire board at a full board meeting. Furthermore, according to his contract, three months notice was required between the official vote to terminate and actual termination of services. With two executive directors and a potential law suit on their hands, the trustees were in a quandary. Three weeks elapsed before the full board could meet to discuss the problem and take a vote on the first executive director's job. During that time, the executive director mobilized considerable support from disgruntled trustees who were angry at the incompetence of the executive committee. During the board meeting, the lawyer for the executive director successfully convinced a majority of trustees to provide six months severance pay for his client, an expense that could have been avoided had the board given proper attention to the bylaws.

In addition to the *Articles of Organization* and the *Bylaws*, some organizations develop two other "rulebooks," one primarily for staff and the other for the board. The staff rulebook is called a *Personnel Manual* and is discussed in detail in Chapter 3. It provides information about hiring and firing, vacation and sick days, leaves, performance and salary reviews, working hours and conditions, and benefits. The board rulebook, or *Trustee Manual*, will be discussed later in this chapter. It provides a more detailed account of the roles and responsibilities of trustees.

The four documents just described provide the trustees with a mechanism for setting broad policy on the *internal* structure and operation of their organization. But they do not deal in much depth with the *external* operation—that is, they do not develop policy concerning the organization's programs and activities. Yet, this is one of the principal functions of a board of trustees.

Trustees must set the course for the organization from year to year by establishing broadly stated "goals."[2] They must also develop specific "objectives" to direct what they want to achieve in a given period of time such as the upcoming year. Once these objectives are set, trustees are additionally responsible for implementing an evaluation process to determine whether the objectives were achieved. (Chapter 4 offers a fuller discussion of these aspects of policy development.)

FISCAL RESPONSIBILITIES

"The executive director really knows about the budget. Let's let him develop the numbers, and we will simply approve what he comes up with." "The staff is honest; let's not make their life complicated by insisting on cumbersome check signing and cash handling procedures."

---

[2]The word *goal* refers to an end toward which certain activities can be directed. For example, it is a goal for the Compton Community Center to provide more opportunities for physical exercise to school children in the city. The term *objective* refers to the means by which the goal is achieved. It is timebound, usually quantitative, and measurable. Thus an objective might be: to provide at least 30 minutes a week of supervised physical activities to 850 children from low-income families.

Many trustees either make statements like these or make decisions that indicate that they believe them. In doing so, they are not only abrogating their responsibility to preserve the public trust by neglecting a fiduciary (or fiscal/financial) responsibility, they are making themselves personally liable for legal action. Many trustees are under the mistaken notion that while a corporation can be sued, an individual who serves on its board is immune and cannot be sued. However, this is not the case. Corporations do offer certain protections, but if creditors want to collect what they feel is rightfully due them, and if the corporation has no assets, creditors may decide to go after the personal assets of the trustees. Whether creditors can collect or not will depend on whether they can prove fiscal negligence on the part of the trustees. If the corporation cannot pay the bill because the trustees did not act responsibly in exercising some kind of financial oversight and control, creditors may persuade the court to allow them to collect from the trustees. At best, the trustees will find themselves having to pay the costs of an attorney; at worst, they will have to pay off the creditors.

The best way for trustees to avoid such a situation is to exercise financial responsibility. This involves developing and monitoring *budgets* on the one hand and establishing *fiscal controls* on the other. In the area of budgets, the trustees perform several functions. One is a planning function. The preparation of the annual budget must be accomplished with the involvement of board members (a finance committee is often assembled for this purpose) and these individuals must satisfy themselves that revenues will be adequate to meet projected expenses. If there is a deficit at the end of the year, the trustees should share the responsibility with the staff. It is simply not sufficient to say: "The executive director was incorrect in his projections." The trustees must also admit: "We did not ask enough probing questions." (Chapter 5 details the steps involved in the budgeting process).

Preparing a budget is only part of the trustee's budgetary responsibility. The two additional trustee functions are *approval* and *monitoring*. The approval step, which must be completed before the budget period begins, is an official action on the part of the trustees that carries the force of an endorsement. It says to the staff: "We have reviewed this budget and are satisfied that revenues and expenditures appear reasonable and achievable. We will take responsibility in helping you meet your revenue targets." Obviously, such a statement indicates that if there are projected revenues based on fund raising, the trustees have implicitly made a commitment to assist in this area.

Approving a budget is not enough. The trustees are responsible for monitoring and, if necessary, amending the budget throughout the year. Financial statements must be prepared for every board meeting that show how the actual revenue and expense figures compare with what has been budgeted (see Figure 2.1).

The example in Figure 2.1 was taken from the first year's operation of the Compton Community Center as an independent corporation. The move to the new building had not yet taken place, and the budget was still modest. In spite of these factors, the trustees of the Compton Community Center received some surprises when they reviewed the financial statement for the first three months of the fiscal year. The left-hand column showed the actual approved annual budget figures; the center column showed receipts and expenditures up to the closing date on the statement; the right-hand column showed the difference between the first two columns for each budget category. At this point in the year, the trustees had an opportunity to assess the various budget estimates and adjust the original budget based on the more up-to-date information given in the financial statement.

The trustees were not pleased with what they saw on this statement. For example, the revenue category called "Grants" showed only $1,000 of income after three months even though $10,000 had been budgeted for the year. One trustee asked whether the original figure was realistic. If not, she suggested that a more modest projection of income be inserted into the original budget; expenditures would then have to be adjusted downward as well. Similarly, the expense categories of telephone, utilities, and office supplies appeared to be considerably under-

FIGURE 2.1. Compton Community Center Three-Month Financial Statement (9/1/79–11/30/79

Revenues	Budget	Year to Date	Balance
Membership	$22,500	$ 6,212	$16,288
Admissions	6,500	2,431	4,069
Contributions	5,000	1,100	3,900
Grants	10,000	1,000	9,000
Total	$44,000	$10,743	$33,257
Expenses			
Salaries	$21,000	$ 5,250	$15,750
Fees/Honoraria	5,000	2,000	3,000
Rent	4,000	1,000	3,000
Telephone	1,000	512	488
Utilities	500	333	167
Office Supplies	800	612	188
Sports Equipment	2,200	1,000	1,200
Benefit Expense	2,000	0	2,000
Educational Program	7,500	3,333	4,167
Total	$44,000	$14,040	$29,960

budgeted given the fact that nine months remained in the fiscal year. To her surprise, the board asked Mary Clarke to make adjustments.

Monitoring the budget is an important responsibility of the trustees, one which establishes certain important financial controls. Other controls can be set through financial policy development. The board must determine such things as:

- Who will approve invoices and sign checks?
- Will individual staff members who are responsible for finances be bonded? Will the treasurer be bonded?
- Will there be a petty cash account and what controls will be put on its use?
- Should the organization allow "first person" checks that are not countersigned?

Answers to each of these questions are given in Chapter 5. It is sufficient to say at this point that there are standard fiscal operating procedures for nonprofit organizations. These are generally known by most accountants and thus it is appropriate that such an individual should serve on the board so that he or she can assist in developing appropriate fiscal policies. In this way, the trustees can assure themselves that the organization's financial house is in order.

FUND RAISING

No group of people should display a greater commitment to a nonprofit organization than its trustees. These individuals, who have agreed to serve the organization in a variety of ways, must set the tone for others—people in the community, funders, constituents, audience members, clients. Trustees must support the organization in spirit, encouraging others to be as enthusiastic about its programs and activities as they are; and they must support the organization more tangibly with money, demonstrating that those closest to the organization, its trustees, are 100 percent committed to it. Put quite simply, *everyone who serves on a board of trustees must contribute some cash every year to their organization.* How much they contribute is another matter, but there should be no ambiguity about the requirement of some sort of annual *cash* gift.

It is not unusual for a potential funder to ask: "What percentage of your trustees contribute to your organization?" This question is a quick way for a donor to garner information on board commitment. If 100 percent of the trustees are contributing, and if 20 percent of the individual donations are coming from the board, then the donor sees a level of commitment that allows him or her to say: "I see there is support from the core group, which gives me confidence to invest in the effort." On the other hand, minimal support can make a donor somewhat suspicious. "If the board is not contributing, why should I? What do they know that I don't?"

In some organizations, the matter of trustee donations is controversial because the trustees are recruited from community groups representing the lower end of the economic scale. The statement that "some people cannot afford to make a donation" is generally a ruse to avoid tackling the issue of required trustee donations head on. There is practically no one sitting on a board of trustees who cannot afford to come up with $10 once a year, and most people can probably come up with $50. If special exceptions have to be made from time to time, they can be considered on a case-by-case basis; this should be no excuse for the absence of a stated policy on board contributions.

How much should trustees be required to give? There is no correct amount and each organization must try to arrive at a formula that seems right and fair. In some organizations, there is no minimum contribution, people simply give what they can but everyone must give something. In other organizations, a guideline rather than a requirement is offered. For example, "This year, our twenty-member board will be expected to contribute $5,000, or an average of $250 per trustee." In still others, a minimum level is set, anywhere from $100 to $2,500 per person. Finally, some organizations set a minimum level, say $300 per person, and state that only half or a third must be contributed in cash and the rest may be contributed in some other form such as help in the office, donated equipment or food, or other forms of volunteer assistance. Keep in mind, though, that trustees are already expected to contribute time to the organization and if volunteer hours are to be counted towards a donation, these should very clearly be "over and above" hours.

In addition to giving money, trustees must help raise money. Each trustee, in fact, should assist in some way with the fund-raising effort. Some will feel uncomfortable doing direct solicitation; but, as we will see in Chapter 8, there are many other tasks involved in fund raising—prospect identification, list development and maintenance, letter writing, planning of events, proposal writing—and every member of the board should be assigned some task related to one of these activities.

In selecting trustees, it is important to recruit people who have contacts in the funding community such as business people, wealthy individuals, and prominent citizens. Some of these people will recoil from the idea of fund raising. "I couldn't possibly ask my friends for money," is a typical refrain. However, these same people may be willing to do other things that are equally valuable. For example, while they may not want to ask their friends for money directly, they may be willing to make appointments for other people in the organization to do it. Or, it is likely that they will at least share their knowledge of these friends' philanthropic interests, which is valuable information as the organization plans how and when to ask them for money. Trustees from the business community may not be willing to solicit their peers but may be willing to give a lunch on the organization's behalf at which contacts can be made, or they may be willing to make a phone call to set up an appointment for the executive director, which will ensure that the request gets past the secretary. Trustees who can "open doors" in this way are as valuable as those who actually do the fund raising.

Ultimately, an organization's list of trustees can itself be part of a fund-raising strategy. While people should not be selected for name value alone—a blue ribbon "name" list can be put together as an advisory committee if "window dressing" is called for—a well-balanced group of influential trustees says something to funders about the importance of the organization in the community. If Mabel, John, and Sam (all prominent citizens) are willing to give their time and their names to this organization, it must be worthy of attention. If, in addition, they are willing to solicit funds on the organization's behalf, it must be worthy of support.

HIRING THE CHIEF EXECUTIVE

The character of almost every nonprofit organization is set in large measure by its chief executive. This is because the chief executive not only speaks for the organization publicly but he or she also hires the staff that deals on a day-to-day basis with the organization's constituency. Thus, the public's impression of the organization is very much in the chief executive's hands. Consequently, the selection of this person is a very great responsibility as is its regular evaluation of his or her performance. In selecting the chief executive, the following rules should be followed.

- Trustees should agree on what their expectations are. They should decide what kind of person they are looking for and what special qualifications the person should possess *before* they look at a single resumé.
- Trustees should document what the job entails. There should be a clear job description (see Chapter 3) that lists both general responsibilities and specific tasks.
- In talking to serious candidates, trustees should be honest about organizational problems. They should not pretend things are fine when they are not. If there are financial problems, staff problems, or even trustee problems, there is nothing to gain in the long run by hiding them.

- Trustees should be clear about how the chief executive's performance is going to be evaluated. If there is a formal review process, it should be described. If there is not, the person should be told what criteria will be used to determine how successfully he or she is doing the job.

Regular evaluation of a chief executive is an excellent way to foster good communication about perceived successes, failures, and expectations for the future. Evaluation should take place at least once a year, at some time immediately prior to the negotiation over salary for the upcoming year. Although Chapter 3 gives general advice on personnel evaluations, one special feature of the chief executive's review should be mentioned here. Unlike most staff members, the chief executive works for more than one person. He or she works for all of the trustees. Thus, the evaluation of a chief executive is not quite as straight-forward as regular staff evaluations. Whatever system is set up, there should be some way for the full board to have input into the process.

One system that seems to work well is for the president of the board to circulate a questionnaire to trustees asking specific questions about the chief executive's performance during the past year. After the responses are collected, the president can then summarize these responses for the chief executive, soliciting his or her reaction. Once the performance review is completed and general job performance objectives are set for the following year, the results are summarized and circulated to the full board for review. After the process is completed, salary negotiation can begin.

Sometimes a board of trustees is faced with the unpleasant task of having to fire a chief executive. Occasionally (though the occasions are few and far between), the person has done something illegal or so blatantly offensive that immediate termination is the only alternative. More often than not though, the situation is more of a judgement call, which makes the decision particularly sensitive and difficult. In spite of this fact, it is always better to "bite the bullet" and address the problem directly rather than to let it fester and hope it will go away. Trustees should never feel guilty about initiating a process of evaluation that may lead to termination. Those who resist doing so are not exercising their responsibility to the organization they are serving.

The "performance review" is a convenient first opportunity to alert the chief executive that the trustees are dissatisfied with his or her performance. The more specific the criticisms at this stage, the easier it will be for the board president to communicate them and to develop a procedure whereby the executive is given some time to try to improve job performance. At the time that the board president speaks to the chief executive, board "concerns" should be communicated *in writing* and written performance objectives should be set for a fixed probationary time period (preferably not more than three months). For example, the board may be concerned that fiscal management is sloppy and that financial statements are always late and inaccurate. A specific performance objective might be that the executive provide monthly financial statements to the board no later than two weeks after the close of each month. These statements can be checked by the board's treasurer. Along with specific job objectives like this, the president should outline the criteria that will be used to judge whether the executive has been able to improve his or her performance on the job. After all of this is explained, the chief executive is given time to evaluate the situation, to try to improve, and to explore other employment opportunities. If, at the end of the period, the executive has not resigned, and the board is still unhappy with job performance, a final opportunity for a resignation should be offered before the board resorts to the more extreme measure of formal termination.

THE COMMUNICATIONS LINK

Many nonprofit organizations are the "best kept secret in town." Others go about their business without the benefit of any input from those they are supposed to be serving. In both cases, the fault lies partly with trustees who do not understand that part of their responsibility is to promote their organization's activities widely and to seek opinions and observations about the organization from a variety of people. Trustees should make regular appearances on behalf of the organization, speaking to community and business groups as well as to friends and associates. Some trustees may be better public speakers than others, but every trustee should take the responsibility to tell people about the organization's activities and its importance to the community. At both formal functions and informal get-togethers, trustees should attempt to set up the two-way communications link with the public; they should provide free publicity and advocacy on behalf of the organization and they should also get feedback from people to find out how others feel about what the organization is doing. Consider the following case.

> During a Rotary luncheon, a trustee of a local music-in-the-schools organization gave a short talk about the upcoming activities for the year, gently suggesting that the Rotarians might wish to make a modest contribution to the program. During the question and answer period, several members of her audience chided her about the seemingly elitist attitude of her program. Why did the group present only classical music? Wasn't jazz an art form too? Why were all the performers from out of state? Didn't their state have any good musicians? After hearing

the reaction of the Rotarians, the trustee discussed the experience with her board. Several substantive changes were made in the program. The following year, the trustee went back to the Rotarians to thank them for their suggestions that had resulted in major changes in the program. The result was a $500 donation from the Rotary.

Because part of the responsibility of trustees is to provide a communications link with the community, it should be clear why it is so important that a diversity of backgrounds be represented on the board. When all segments of the community are represented, each group sees the organization as its own and this increases support in many tangible and intangible ways.

STAYING WITHIN THE LAW

Nonprofit organizations have to follow many rules and regulations set by federal, state, and local governments. Assuming that they have a modest amount of financial activity, they must file financial reports with the United States Internal Revenue Service (Form 990) and with the state office handling public charities. They must fill out tax forms for employees, deduct taxes from paychecks, and deposit these funds periodically in an account at a local bank. They have to keep personnel records and may have to pay into a state unemployment insurance fund. They must maintain minutes of board meetings, keep updated copies of the Bylaws and Articles of Organization, and file a number of other documents with various agencies, often on an annual basis. While staff members are generally responsible for actually doing the work, the trustees must monitor these activities for compliance and completeness. It is essential to remember that as stewards of the public trust, the trustees are responsible for overseeing compliance with legal requirements.

One of the most serious oversights in this area centers around withholding taxes. A surprisingly large number of nonprofit organizations fail to make payments of withholding taxes on time; some fail to do so altogether and end up spending the government's tax money on other things. When the federal and state authorities discover this, they have little sympathy. Not only do they demand what is due them, but they charge interest on the monies not paid. The impact on the budget of a nonprofit organization can be devastating. While staff members can walk away from the situation with nothing lost but their jobs and perhaps their reputations (and sometimes not even that), trustees are left to deal with the financial mess. For these reasons, even the smallest nonprofit organization should have one lawyer and one accountant on the board. These people should be assigned the task of monitoring the legal and financial activities of the organization.

BOARD COMPOSITION

The responsibilities of trustees previously detailed suggest those skills and areas of knowledge that a board must collectively possess. A practical listing might include the following areas of expertise.

— nonprofit trusteeship
— legal matters
— financial/accounting
— fund raising (including: business/corporate, individual, public agency, foundation)
— personnel management
— public relations

Trustees should also be familiar with the programs and activities that the organization sponsors, and all trustees should support the organization's mission. They should represent a variety of different backgrounds as well as various segments of the community, including different minority and ethnic groups that will give the board a broad vision and understanding of the true meaning of community and public service. In addition, specific nonprofits may require trustees with other types of expertise and representation. For example, if a nonprofit corporation owns a facility, operates a building, or maintains extensive grounds, it may be desirable to have an architect or a contractor on the board.

The purpose of having trustees with specific expertise is not to encourage encroachment on day-to-day activities that are the staff's responsibility but to provide a monitoring capability for the board. Such trustee expertise helps the board in formulating policy, reacting to staff recommendations, and choosing between alternate courses of action.

When choosing fellow trustees, the tendency is to say, "My friend John is interested in what we do, and he has served on the governing board of our church. I think he would be excellent." But this approach is not systematic enough and does not give enough consideration to the kinds of specific expertise that the board requires. An interest in an organization is not sufficient.

For this reason, the development of a *skills inventory chart* is an excellent and simple mechanism for forcing the board (through its nominating committee, and with staff, when appropriate) to analyze its needs. A skills inventory chart lists specific skills down the left-hand margin and lists existing and potential board members along the top axis.

Looking at Figure 2.2, we can see how it can be used. In this specific case, it is clear, first, that none of the existing trustees (Jones,

	Jones	Smith	Brown	Fox	Evans	etc.
legal						
accounting		X				
corporate fund raising						
public relations			X			
music performance				X		
personnel						
facility management					X	

FIGURE 2.2.

Smith, Brown, Fox, and Evans) bring expertise in the legal field, in personnel, or in corporate fund raising. As the organization looks for new trustees, people with skills and experience in these areas should be sought. Second, we can see that Jones does not appear to be pulling his weight according to the skill areas listed. He may be on the board for other valid reasons, but the organization should analyze carefully what these reasons are. Third, while Smith (the organization's treasurer and a certified public accountant) brings considerable expertise in the financial/accounting area, her term is due to expire. If she is not re-elected to the board, it will be necessary to find someone with similar skills to replace her.

THE DEADWOOD PROBLEM

Regardless of how hard a nominating committee may work, there will always be some board members who are not pulling their weight, are not active, and are not contributing either financially or otherwise to the organization. While this "deadwood problem" will almost always exist to a certain extent, there are things that can be done to minimize it.

LIMITING TERMS OF OFFICE

No trustee should assume that he or she is going to serve the organization indefinitely. Limits should be placed on terms of office and on the number of times a trustee can be re-elected. One system that seems to work well is to have a three-year term with one opportunity for re-election. After three years, a trustee comes up for re-election; after six, he or she must go off the board for at least one year before being invited to serve again. Trustee rotation offers a process for replacing weak board members with enthusiastic and committed trustees. Since continuity on the board is important, though, it is desirable to stagger the terms of trustees so that only one third of the board members should be reaching the end of their terms in any one year.

ATTENDANCE

Nothing undermines the effectiveness of a board more than absence from meetings. Participation by everyone is necessary if the board is going to operate effectively. Thus, it should be a stated policy of the organization that attendance at board meetings is required. Beyond this, the board might adopt a policy that two unexcused absences in a year constitute an automatic resignation. If a trustee has a legitimate problem, such as an illness or a death in the family, the president can excuse that trustee from a meeting. However, without such a legitimate excuse (and without approval of the president), the policy should be clear that the trustee is expected to be at all board meetings. A slightly more liberal policy might be developed for attendance at committee meetings.

FINANCIAL COMMITMENT

Previously it was pointed out that a nonprofit organization should insist that every trustee make an annual cash contribution. This contribution requirement, as well as the other obligations of trusteeship, must be clearly articulated to potential trustees as part of the recruitment and invitation process. The "pocketbook test" is, in fact, one excellent way to separate those who will demonstrate commitment to the organization from those who will not.

THE TRUSTEE MANUAL

The "deadwood problem" is most prevalent when trustees lack a thorough understanding of the responsibilities of trusteeship and when they have the impression that serving on a board is more of a social function than a business function. To combat this problem, every organization should develop a *Trustee Manual*. Such a manual should be presented in loose-leaf form so that it can be updated regularly. The manual should include the following sections.

- Articles of Organization with Mission Statement (The actual incorporation papers are less critical than the language that defines the nature and function of the organization.)

- Bylaws (Bylaws are usually divided into "Sections"; each of these sections should begin on a new page to facilitate scanning for specific information.)
- List of current trustees with business and home addresses, phone numbers, and term expiration dates.
- List of committees and their respective members.
- List of staff members with titles and areas of responsibility.
- Brief (2–3 page) history of the organization.
- Description of roles, responsibilities, and requirements of trustees (This section should summarize the kind of information contained in this chapter relating to general trustee responsibilities; it should then state the specific requirements—attendance, financial contribution, committee responsibility—that will be expected of everyone.)
- Minutes of current fiscal year meetings.
- Specific planning documents if available (A series of goals statements is often included here.)
- The annual report from the last completed fiscal year (An annual report generally includes the audited financial statements. In lieu of an annual report, a promotional booklet can be submitted along with the financial statements.)

RECRUITMENT AND ORIENTATION

Related to the need for a *Trustee Manual* is a complementary need for both a clear recruitment procedure (which spells out the roles and responsibilities of trustees) and an orientation session for individuals who have agreed to join the board. Following is the process.

- A nominating committee is set up (with members either elected by the board or appointed by the president).
- The committee analyzes board needs, evaluates the performance of trustees up for re-election, solicits names of other prospective trustees, and reviews a prospective slate with the full board.
- After tentative and initial approval of the slate, appointments are made with prospective trustees. Each individual is visited by at least one member of the board (often the president) who is sometimes accompanied by the executive director. At the meeting, the roles, responsibilities, and requirements of trusteeship are described. A copy of the trustee manual is left with the person so that he or she may study it in detail before making his or her decision. (If the person elects not to serve on the board, the trustee manual should be returned).
- No more than one week after the visit, the prospective trustee should be asked for a final decision. If the answer is "yes," then the individual will have to be officially elected to the board according to the process set out in the bylaws.
- Once a year, the board should hold an orientation session. If held at the organization's office, the session can provide new trustees with the

opportunity to meet the staff and observe the daily operations. The president, executive director, and committee chairs often give a series of short and informal speeches and, in some cases, an outside "expert" provides a "pep talk" on trustee roles and responsibilities. An orientation session is sometimes arranged to coincide with an event sponsored by the organization.

EVALUATION AND DISMISSAL

Some organizations have a formal review period at the end of each year at which time trustees evaluate one another's performance. It is usually the president who determines the evaluation process. Among the options available are informal discussions with each trustee or anonymous written statements. Whatever the process, the objective is the same: to identify ineffective trustees. If the president discovers that a trustee consistently receives poor evaluations from fellow board members, it is time to take action. Dismissal, through a majority vote of the board or some other procedure, is an action that should only be taken in the case of gross misconduct. However, other more moderate methods may lead to the same outcome. For example, a strong president can often counsel a trustee to resign by suggesting that he or she is overcommitted or seems to have lost interest.

It should be remembered that a good rotation policy through limited terms of office often makes the issue of trustee dismissal and forced resignation moot. Since terms are limited, most boards can live with a "do nothing" trustee for a year, or two, or even three. On self-perpetuating boards, however, where terms are not fixed, evaluation, dismissal, and resignation become more critical.

COMMITTEES

When a nonprofit organization reaches a certain size and its operation becomes more complex, the board usually finds that it is difficult to carry out all of its responsibilities efficiently without dividing up into smaller groups. These groups, or committees, allow for a detailed analysis of specific areas like fund raising, planning, budgeting or programs, before they are discussed by the full board. A committee structure offers several advantages: first, it allows for a division of the work load; second, it promotes a more informal discussion of the pros and cons of various issues before they come to the board for a formal resolution; third, it allows an organization to bring experts into the deliberation process without putting them on the board. For example, a fund-raising committee may be composed of a representative from the business community who is glad to help on an occasional basis but does not have the time or the inclination to be a trustee. In general, a committee should be chaired by a trustee and the majority of committee members should be board members, but outside resource people and staff members can and should be included because they are often an asset.

The following committees are common in nonprofit organizations.

Executive: This committee is generally empowered to act for the full board in matters that require immediate action and/or do not involve major questions of policy or funding. It is also the chief coordinating committee for the board, mapping out how the board's business should be conducted, setting agendas, and organizing the activity of other committees. The executive director will often use the Executive Committee as a "troubleshooting" group, bringing to it problems needing rapid resolution. Generally the corporation's officers (president, treasurer, clerk, and any other officers that may be named) serve on this committee.

Finance: This committee is headed by the treasurer and is empowered to study and make recommendations regarding all financial procedures and controls, assist in the preparation and presentation of budgets, and review all financial statements. An accountant is invaluable on this committee.

Development: This committee oversees the planning and coordination of fund-raising efforts.

Nominating: This committee identifies, screens, and recommends prospective trustees. Members of this committee can also assist in the recruitment and orientation of the trustees.

Planning: This committee coordinates long-range planning. Its function is described in detail in Chapter 4.

Buildings and Grounds: For organizations that own or manage facilities or property, this committee will monitor their condition, recommend maintenance and repairs, and plan renovation projects. It is advisable to have an architect or someone with similar expertise on this committee.

Public Relations: Many nonprofit organizations have not developed a well-conceived approach to public relations and find themselves "the best kept secret in town." For those organizations, and for others that sell a service or a product, it may be important to have a committee that can plan and oversee a public relations strategy. On such a public relations committee, it is often useful to have someone from the media or from a public relations firm.

Events or *Benefit:*   Organizations planning special events generally delegate responsibility for them to a special committee. Fund-raising events, such as benefits, should be handled by this committee, not the development committee.

Program: This committee is organized to review the program activities of the organization and plan for the future. Because this committee has to work very closely with staff, its members must take care not to meddle in areas better left to staff management.

Personnel: This committee develops personnel policies (see Chapter 3), recommends salary ranges to the board, may evaluate the executive director and recommend a specific salary level for that individual, reviews benefit packages, and handles grievances when board involvement is necessary.

Few organizations will have all of these committees, and some organizations will have committees not listed here. Committees should only be formed if and when there is a need for them. Committee meetings, like board meetings, should have tight agendas and should not waste people's time.

OFFICERS

State law generally requires that a nonprofit corporation's board of trustees include at least three officers: a president (or chairman/chairperson), a treasurer, and a clerk (or secretary). Some organizations include additional officers, such as a vice president or an assistant treasurer. The organization's bylaws will specify how many officers there must be, their titles, powers, and duties. The bylaws will also state the process by which they are elected and the frequency of the elections. (In this connection, it is common practice for the board to elect officers from among its ranks at the annual meeting of the corporation.) The selection of the right people to fill officer positions is an important task. Only the most qualified trustees should be considered for the regular officer positions. No one should be appointed to any of the three crucial positions (president, treasurer, clerk) simply as an honor. It is an acceptable practice for an organization to create "honorary" officer positions such as "honorary chairperson" or "president emeritus" (to honor a past president who is no longer active), so long as it is clear that these people have no special powers.

President: The president should be a person of authority who is respected by the board, the staff, the community, and has plenty of time to devote to the job. He or she should serve on the executive committee for at least a year before assuming the presidency in order to become thoroughly familiar with the operation of the organization. A good president can set the work standard for the board that keeps the "deadwood" problem to a minimum and keeps the trustees on track with their tasks in board and committee work. A good president can serve as a buffer between disgruntled trustees and the executive director, mediating tensions and resolving differences. A weak president, on the other hand, may allow various factions to secure for themselves too much authority and control. Personal agendas may then take precedence over organizational priorities. No one should be appointed to the presidency who is afraid to deal firmly with those who are getting out of line.

Treasurer: The treasurer must be someone with a good deal of financial experience, preferably in the operation of nonprofit organizations. Accountants and business people are generally preferred for this job; however, many of these individuals who have only profit-sector experience, are not sensitive to the special characteristics of financial management in the nonprofit sector, which are discussed in Chapter 5. It is advantageous to find a person with some board experience in another nonprofit organization who also has the financial expertise to head a finance committee.

Clerk: The clerk (or secretary) must be well organized and have the ability to record information accurately. The clerk's task is important to the extent that he or she is responsible for maintaining the official records of meetings. For each meeting, the clerk must send out the agenda and keep the minutes. Unless meetings are tape-recorded, the minutes will be the only official record of board deliberation, and consequently they *must* reproduce the *actual* words of motions, who made and seconded them, and how they were voted. It is less important to keep a record of extended discussion on any particular issue, and the clerk should focus primarily on the decisions themselves. Once minutes are written, they should be circulated so that the trustees have a chance to review them in preparation for approval at the subsequent board meeting. If corrections are needed, a board member makes a motion to amend a certain section. After all the corrections are complete, the trustees vote to accept the minutes. With this vote, the minutes become part of the corporate records. The importance of the minutes cannot be overstated. Once they are approved, no board or staff member can claim that "things really did not happen that way at the meeting." They constitute the official and binding record of board decisions.

SUMMARY

Five years after Mary Clarke had assembled her first board of trustees, she decided to find out why she was having such problems with the group. She went to an experienced trustee from another organization and asked for his views on trusteeship. After getting a long briefing on the roles and responsibilities of trustees, their various obligations, the commitment and time and money they should be expected to make, Mary asked: "Why would anyone want to serve on a Board?"

The answer to Mary's question is that trusteeship is a form of public service that often carries with it status in the community. Many established nonprofit organizations find people vying for the chance to become trustees. These are the lucky ones. For many of the newer, less prestigious organizations, finding committed trustees is more difficult. Nevertheless, these organizations should not compromise and turn the board into a social group with minimal responsibilities because eventually, as the organization grows in prominence and importance, weak trustees become a tremendous liability. It is better to take great care, to move slowly and carefully, even if it takes several years to achieve the full complement of trustees. In the long run, the safe and prudent course is to build soundly for the organization's future.

3
The Staff

As a group, people who are interested in working for nonprofit organizations are often creative, enthusiastic, and fun to talk with. Sometimes, they come with considerable training and background in the field in which the organization is active such as education, medicine, social service, politics, and the arts. Often they are willing to accept low wages in order to be able to work with other interesting people in an environment that is not as impersonal or inflexible as a large corporate office. Unfortunately, however, what the prospective worker may bring in enthusiasm and creativity, he or she often lacks in management skills. The nonprofit organization usually needs experienced managers with business, financial, and even legal skills; it needs clerical workers and data processing professionals who are familiar with the workings of an office and the needs of administrators. The pool of applicants for jobs in nonprofit organizations, however, is usually heavily weighted in favor of those with a more generalized liberal arts training.

This poses serious problems for the executive of the nonprofit organization who is attempting to fill staff positions. Should the executive hire someone who is bright and may be able to learn quickly on the job? Should the executive count as experience an applicant's general knowledge of and interest in the field in which the organization is active? Should the executive hire someone with a Ph.D. for a low-level clerical job if the applicant seems willing? What are the long-term implications of staffing a nonprofit organization with people whose primary knowledge pool does not include administration.

In order to answer these questions, it is first necessary to distinguish between program personnel and management personnel. Obviously, if a mental health center is hiring a psychiatrist, it will look for one who is well trained and knowledgeable in *psychology;* if a theater troupe is hiring actors for a stage production, the people selected must have dramatic talent; if a school is hiring a teacher, a strong educational background is a primary prerequisite if not the paramount consideration. Certainly in staffing the *programmatic* side of a nonprofit organization, direct training, experience, and skill in the field of activity is the primary criterion by which people should initially be judged.

However, on the management side, the issue is not so clear. Might we speculate that an accountant with a knowledge of biology will do a better job of keeping the books for a hospital than someone without such knowledge? Will a clerk/typist who is also a painter be expected to perform better than an ordinary secretary if the employer happens to run an art gallery? Or, more generally, should recruitment procedures in nonprofit organizations give preference to those whose backgrounds are somehow related to the programmatic activity of the organization?

The answers to all these questions is probably "no." When

looking for a bookkeeper or a secretary, the most important consideration is the person's skill *at that job*. In some cases, in fact, it may be preferable to hire someone without a special interest in the organization's field of activity because there is less likelihood that the individual will feel frustrated in performing menial tasks. It is also less likely that the employee will possess a driving ambition to move up and/or out to a more interesting, program-related job. The controversy surrounding this point among nonprofit administrators is keen. But more often than not, experienced executives tend to favor entry-level and middle management personnel with strong backgrounds in administrative areas.

EXPECTATIONS

Keep in mind that some people think of nonprofit organizations as places full of interesting people who work in a loose and nonhierarchical administrative structure. While this may attract creative people, it also tends to attract those who are suspicious of authority and of hierarchically arranged organizations. Individuals who come from a management background, on the other hand, tend to be more familiar and comfortable with organizational hierarchies. Often they have worked for profit-making concerns where hierarchies are set in concrete. As nonprofit organizations grow in complexity and size, they must move toward increasingly hierarchical structures. If they are staffed primarily by people who believe in collective decision making, or who feel that all supervision should be informal and unstructured, then dissension, frustration, and unhappiness can quickly set in.

Another major misconception about nonprofit organizations is that administrative jobs within them tend to be more interesting than comparable jobs in the profit sector. By and large, this is not the case. An unsuccessful candidate for political office should not look to a bookkeeping job in a university's public administration graduate school as a way to work off his or her disappointment and frustrations. An unemployed musician or painter who looks to an arts organization as a way to satisfy his or her creative needs is likely to be equally unhappy. "Administration," says one nonprofit executive, "is the art of pushing paper. If you enjoy doing that task well, if you like inventing better systems for making the paper pushing more efficient, you can satisfy your needs. But do not look for great emotional satisfactions."

Finally, it is not true that a nonprofit organization is a haven from the real workaday world dominated by profit-motivated corporations, big government, and a largely impersonal, insensitive, and inflexible work environment. While there is a grain of truth here, it is remarkable how rapidly nonprofit organizations have become integrated into the world they are supposed to be unlike. Nonprofits that find themselves competing to sell a service or a product, to influence public policy, or to secure funding, find the going very competitive and the pressure at times tremendous. Nonprofit organizations must work with government agencies at the local, state, and federal levels to preserve tax exemptions, secure funding, and manage personnel records, to name just a few such functions. Nonprofit organizations are very much a part of the corporate/governmental structure as many employees discover to their unhappiness.

CREATIVITY/FLEXIBILITY

It would be misleading to suggest that the best nonprofit employees are nose-to-the-grindstone management types without any sensitivity or interest in their organization's activities and without any imagination. Obviously, all other things being equal, an executive should certainly give preference to an applicant who, along with management skills, brings a knowledge, aptitude, and/or interest in other fields, particularly those related to the organization's mission. Even more important, however, may be the quality of imagination and flexibility that the person brings to the organization that allows him or her to grow in the job and help shape it and make it more productive.

Unlike large corporations that are highly structured and in which roles are carefully defined and largely unchanging, the nonprofit organization is usually small enough and sufficiently understaffed that a single person may be called upon to fill a number of roles and perform a variety of tasks. In addition, because the administrative needs of the organization can change quickly through rapid growth or equally rapid constriction, a person hired to perform one constellation of tasks may be asked to consider a reassignment of responsibilities. Volatility and change is common among nonprofits and, as a consequence, flexibility in employees is an asset. Nonprofit organizations, with the exception of the oldest and most established, are not the place for people who want to know that the job that they are taking today will be the same job ten years hence. Rather, they are good places for people who see organizational change as an opportunity to learn new skills and possibly to secure rapid job advancement.

It is here, in the area of creativity and flexibility, that someone with a broader educational background and varied experience may have a substantial advantage over someone with fairly narrow training and experience in management. In many instances, it will be advantageous to have a person who has, in addition to some administrative skills, an interest in growing with a job and shaping that job into something exciting and challenging. This is not true in every case, of course, because many jobs in nonprofits are routine. However, the nonprofit executive should consider searching out people who appear to have the special spark of curiosity, energy, and creativity even when their management skills are not fully developed.

To summarize: The nonprofit executive must look for several qualities in prospective employees. In order of importance these may be summarized as follows.

1. Management skills related to the job to be performed.
2. Character traits that reflect creativity, flexibility, an enthusiasm for solving problems, and an ability to work with others.
3. An understanding of the need for authority in an organizational structure but not the acceptance of all authority without question.
4. A knowledge, sensitivity, and enjoyment of the nonprofit field in which they will be employed.

SETTING THE ORGANIZATIONAL PARAMETERS

Many organizations are anxious to begin recruiting and hiring staff before they have set basic organizational parameters. Both new organizations filling positions for the first time, and older organizations replacing departing staff, should not rush into the hiring process. Whether it is the trustees hiring the executive director, or the director hiring other staff,[1] organizational parameters have to be set in five areas by:

1. Determining specific tasks.
2. Distributing those tasks among salaried employees, independent contractors, and volunteers.
3. Preparing an organization chart showing chains of command and lines of responsibility.

---

[1]Generally, the board of trustees hires the executive director. The executive director hires other staff. In large organizations where staffs are sizable, division heads usually hire the people that work under them. In the most decentralized organizations, where each employee is hired by his or her immediate supervisor, it is advisable to involve staff colleagues working in the same department in the recruitment and interviewing process. No matter what hiring procedure is used, it is always advantageous to have more than one person forming an impression of prospective employees even if one person ultimately will make the final selection.

4. Writing job descriptions.
5. Deciding on compensation levels and specific benefits.[2]

DETERMINING TASKS

At least annually, or more often if there are significant changes requiring a reshuffling of personnel, the executive director (with the assistance of the board) must list all the tasks that need to get done in the organization. Objectivity is important and the group should not simply be guided by the way things have been in the past. Rather, people should ask themselves the following series of questions.

- What tasks are being performed now and are they absolutely necessary?
- What tasks are not being performed that should be?
- What new activities are being added that will require additional work? What tasks are associated with these activities?
- Where does there currently appear to be the most staff dissatisfaction with job definition? To what extent should the organization redefine the tasks in this area?

In large organizations, this step, together with the ones that follow, may be carried out more effectively with the help of an outside consultant. The consultant brings a kind of objectivity to the process that can be refreshing. Whether or not a consultant is used, employees should be interviewed throughout this process because they have the most expertise about the jobs they perform.

DISTRIBUTING TASKS AMONG SALARIED STAFF, INDEPENDENT CONTRACTORS, AND VOLUNTEERS

Many trustees and staff members make the mistake of assuming that all of the important tasks in a nonprofit organization need to be done by salaried staff. Often this is the most expensive way of getting jobs done and not always the most efficient. For example, consider three nonprofit organizations of roughly comparable size that are faced with the need to maintain their fiscal records.

- Organization A has put a bookkeeper on staff, at a salary of $15,000, who records all transactions, reconciles the bank statement, prepares finan-

---

[2]The term *benefits* as used here may include but is not limited to: vacations, sick days, personal days, maternity and paternity leaves, other leaves of absence, medical insurance, retirement benefits including social security, life insurance, disability insurance, and other forms of nonsalaried compensation. Workman's Compensation and unemployment insurance, while benefiting the employee, are not legally considered "benefits" because they are the employee's right by law.

cial statements for the board, computes all withholding taxes, issues the payroll checks, prepares W-2 forms for employees and 1099 forms for independent contractors. She also prepares the Form 990 on an annual basis for the Internal Revenue Service. This employee is costing the organization a good deal more than $15,000. In addition to her salary, the organization is paying its share of her social security taxes as well as her medical and disability benefits, sick time, holidays, and vacation days, Workman's Compensation, and State Unemployment Insurance.[3] Finally, it provides her with office space and furniture. Thus, the real cost of this employee is close to $20,000.

- Organization B has hired a bookkeeping service at $15,000 a year. The service not only provides all the services that Organization A's bookkeeper performs, but it also computerizes all the records and makes available various kinds of reports that the executive director and the board can use for budgeting and reporting purposes. The service constantly updates all changes in tax laws, accounting procedures relating to nonprofits, and provides free advice that is quite useful. The service requires no office space—records are picked up and delivered—requires no employee benefits, and is entitled to no unemployment benefits (hence Organization B is not liable for unemployment insurance).

- Organization C has taken care of the fiscal area in still a different way. One of the trustees, a retired accountant, has agreed to serve as treasurer. He volunteers his time to the organization, writing checks, preparing financial statements, and helping the executive director with budgets. A staff member, who costs the organization $20,000 a year ($15,000 in salary and $5,000 in benefits, office space, and so on), spends about 20 percent of his time assisting the treasurer with the paper work, filing, record keeping, and so on. Finally, at the treasurer's request, the organization has contracted a "Payroll Service" at a local bank. The service handles all of the payroll-related activity including the collecting of W-4 forms, the computation of deductions, the issuing of checks (as well as automatic depositing into employee accounts where this is requested), and the preparation of W-2 forms at the end of the year. Organization C's total cost is approximately $7,500.

As can be readily seen, organization A, by opting to assign a full-time staff member to the bookkeeping tasks, chose the most expensive alter-

---

[3]Employees of nonprofit organizations are automatically covered by unemployment insurance. The organization itself, however, must be careful to understand its options and liabilities. At the federal level, the organization is exempt from paying unemployment taxes (FUTA). At the state level, however, the organization usually has an option. If state unemployment insurance (usually assessed as a percentage of the employee's salary) is paid regularly, and the employee is subsequently laid off, the state pays the unemployment compensation and the organization pays nothing. If the organization does not pay into the state unemployment insurance fund (and nonprofit organizations usually have this option of not participating in the system), and the employee is laid off or fired, the state pays the unemployment benefit and then charges the organization the full cost of the claim. Nonprofit organizations that are virtually certain they will have no employees collecting unemployment may decide not to pay into the system. Others may wish to. Still others may wish to establish their own *self-insurance fund*, putting aside a certain portion of the employees' salaries into a separate bank account for a time until they feel confident that they are protected against unemployment liability. (*Note:* Unemployment benefits cover only salaried employees, not independent contractors).

native. It would have been desirable for the board of trustees and the executive director to have considered other alternatives before hiring a full-time salaried bookkeeper. Outside service bureaus, volunteers, and part-time or occasional help are sometimes much less expensive and far more efficient. Individuals hired on this basis can always be hired as *independent contractors.*[4] The organization pays them a flat rate for the job, does not need to withhold taxes from their salary, does not offer them benefits, is not liable for social security taxes or unemployment compensation, and is required to file only one form (the Form 1099 at the end of the calendar year), and that only if the employee earns over $600.

PREPARING THE ORGANIZATION CHART

Many nonprofit organizations resist preparing an organization chart. This is probably sensible when there are two or three employees. When there are five or more employees, however, an organization chart becomes a necessity. It establishes chains of authority, lines of responsibility and of reporting. It also establishes lines of accountability.

In a large organization, the executive director must delegate some of his or her authority. Supervision of each and every employee is not possible. However, in delegating authority, the executive director must also delegate accountability. The organization chart in Figure 3.1, for example, tells us to whom the executive director has delegated supervisory authority and who must be spoken to if things go awry.

Consider what would happen in this organization if the executive director received a computer print-out that was full of incorrect information. The director of administration would be called in to discuss the problem. The director of administration, in turn, would take up the problem with the data processing manager who would call in the appropriate D/P clerk responsible for the incorrect input. What the executive director should not do (unless the supervisor has been informed and approves) is to deal directly with the D/P clerk in trying to find out why the print-out was incorrect. This undermines the authority both of the data processing manager and the director of administration and leaves them uninformed about the problem. The executive director may wish to be in attendance when the director of administration talks to the data

---

[4]It is always desirable to have a written contract with an independent contractor that specifies the task to be accomplished, the start date, the end date, and the compensation level. The contract usually should not specify the place where the work will be performed, the work hours, or any other conditions that would suggest that this person is being treated like a regular employee. Keep in mind that the Internal Revenue Service can, and sometimes does, check to see whether independent contractors are actually salaried employees. If the work is short-term, part-time, and if the individual enjoys more independence than other regular employees, the IRS is usually satisfied. If he or she does not fit the definition of an independent contractor, the organization is liable for back taxes not withheld. For this reason, the advice of an accountant or a lawyer in the hiring of independent contractors is desirable.

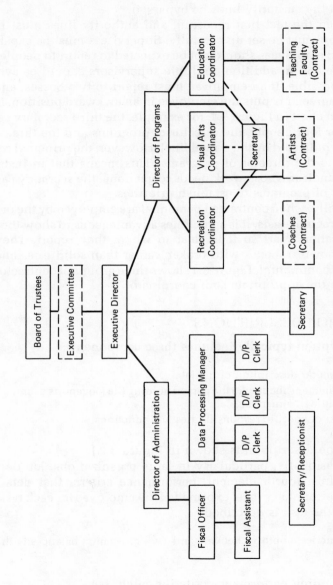

FIGURE 3.1. Organizational Structure for the Compton Community Center

Board of Trustees

Executive Committee

Executive Director

Director of Administration

Director of Programs

Secretary

Fiscal Officer

Fiscal Assistant

Data Processing Manager

D/P Clerk

D/P Clerk

D/P Clerk

Secretary/Receptionist

Recreation Coordinator

Coaches (Contract)

Visual Arts Coordinator

Secretary

Artists (Contract)

Education Coordinator

Teaching Faculty (Contract)

processing manager or when the manager talks to the D/P clerk; or, the executive director may request a meeting in which all are present. In no case should the authority lines be bypassed.

Given the fact that reporting and authority lines must be respected, they must be set up carefully. Supervisors must be capable of supervision; employees should not be expected to report to people who are incompetent. In addition, multiple supervisors should be avoided whenever possible. If an employee must report to two bosses, and the two do not agree, this puts the employee in an awkward position. In the organization chart in Figure 3.1, for example, the third secretary carries out work for four people, the director of programs and the three coordinators (as indicated by the dotted line). However, the principal reporting line is to the director of programs. This means that in instances where it is unclear whose work needs to get done, the secretary can ask the director of programs to establish priorities.

Finally, when contracted personnel are employed by the organization on a regular basis, it is sometimes advantageous to show them on the organization chart so it is clear to whom they report. They are generally shown in boxes with broken rather than solid lines and are indicated as *contractual*. Figure 3.1 shows three groups of contractors all reporting to the appropriate staff coordinator.

WRITING JOB DESCRIPTIONS

A job description typically includes three components:

- A general description of the job.
- A statement about who the person holding the job reports to and who he or she will supervise.
- A list of specific responsibilities and functions.

(A sample job description is shown in Figure 3.2.)

Occasionally, particularly in large organizations, job descriptions contain a fourth element, performance criteria that detail the minimum performance level expected of the employee for each task. For example, if the task is described as:

- reconciles monthly checking and savings account balances with bank statement,

the corresponding performance criterion might be:

- minimum performance standards will have been met if employee presents reconciled statements to supervisor within two weeks of receipt of monthly bank statements.

FIGURE 3.2. Sample Job Description

DATA PROCESSING AND FISCAL ASSISTANT

The data processing and fiscal assistant is generally responsible for the thorough and accurate maintenance of the program and fiscal computer files of the Compton Community Center. He/she is also responsible for the preparation of certain fiscal documents and forms and for the maintenance of related paper files.

The data processing and fiscal assistant reports to the director of administration. He/she supervises a part-time clerk who is hired on an occasional basis to handle extraordinary work load situations.

RESPONSIBILITIES AND FUNCTIONS

Programs
- Reviews and codes all information questionnaires
- Updates and maintains all directories through preparation of appropriate input forms
- Codes report forms for computer input
- Prepares and maintains all evaluation reports
- Reviews computer edit reports and documents all necessary changes
- Maintains master file code records, paper files for questionnaires, office copies of computer edits, master-file printouts and reports.

Fiscal
- Prepares receipt and disbursement reports and general ledgers for all cost centers and accounts; prepares related computer input forms
- Reconciles monthly checking and savings account balances with bank statement
- Processes incoming invoices following assignment of accounting codes by director of administration
- Maintains paper files for all current and historic invoice records
- Maintains computerized cost center file, chart of accounts and vendor file
- Maintains paper files for contracts, insurance policies, and other material pertinent to the fiscal administration of the Compton Community Center

---

Although performance criteria may be useful in very large organizations in which there are routine jobs with predictable tasks, they are usually cumbersome for smaller organizations. Unless it is difficult to evaluate employee performance without them, or unless the situation requires that specific performance criteria be developed while an employee is on probation, doing without them may be preferable.

Why have job descriptions at all? There are many arguments against them. They often take a long time to write and require extensive discussions with staff and several drafts. Furthermore, every time there is a staff reorganization with a shifting of responsibilities, the job descriptions have to be redrafted. Why not spend the time on something more productive and just explain to new staff what they are expected to do when they are hired? There are three reasons why it is important to have job descriptions.

First, the very process of writing job descriptions often reveals that the job responsibilities envisioned for a single person are unrealistic. The executive director and the trustees may agree that one person should staff the development/fund-raising area, for example, but once each and every task is detailed in the job description, it may become apparent that no one person could possibly do all of them. In addition, once all the tasks are written down, it becomes easier to juggle responsibilities with a clearer sense of the total work needs of the organization and the time commitments of each staff member.

Second, job descriptions protect the organization's employees. Employees are able to refer to a document that outlines what is expected of them and provides the basis for an evaluation of their job performance. They cannot be dismissed for not performing a task not mentioned in the job description. Commonly, an employee can expect to be consulted before changes are made in a job description, particularly if the change involves the carrying out of additional tasks. Similarly, the employee's supervisor owes him or her an explanation when tasks detailed in the job description are taken away and given to others. Finally, the employee can expect any job review, particularly one leading to salary adjustments, to be based on an assessment of performance of the tasks listed in the job description.

Third, job descriptions protect the organization. Like contracts, a job description outlines certain expectations *in writing* which, if not lived up to, offer grounds for dismissal. Without a job description, an employee can always say, "But no one ever told me I was supposed to do that." With the written document, there can be no disputing that the responsibilities were spelled out clearly. Similarly, as the supervisor assesses the job performance of an employee at the time of a performance review, he or she has a clear set of tasks and responsibilities to exercise evaluative judgement upon. It helps the supervisor to be objective and to resist the temptation of giving a good evaluation to an employee simply because he or she was quiet or pleasant and a negative evaluation to a less personable or friendly member of the staff.

Many organizations have job descriptions. However, they are often out of date. Typically, an organization will hire a consultant to write job descriptions and then forget that the descriptions need updating as new tasks and jobs are added and responsibilities change. Updating does not have to be difficult and should be done regularly. A certain time can be set aside at least once a year for the executive director (or his or her assistant) to review all job descriptions and recommend changes to the board.

DECIDING ON COMPENSATION LEVELS

Deciding on salary levels and benefits for employees of nonprofit organizations often leads to controversy. Trustees encounter many complicating factors when determining salaries and benefits. For one thing, the organization can be faced with difficult financial obstacles. There is a limit to the amount of money that can be earned and raised. In addition, because it is well known that people are willing to make financial sacrifices in order to work in the nonprofit sector, there may be a great temptation to keep salaries as low as possible. Finally, a nonprofit organization is often staffed by people who are emotionally invested in its mission and whose primary motivations are not financial. This *psychic income* phenomenon is particularly common for founder-directors who are willing to accept an inadequate financial compensation if there is a chance to witness a vision being turned into a reality.

Up until the 1950s, many nonprofit organizations were staffed largely with volunteers and/or independently affluent people who were paid modest salaries. With increased professionalization, conditions have changed, but nonprofit administrators are still, on average, underpaid for the kinds of jobs they do. In some ways this is good for the organizations and their boards. An organization finds itself with plenty of applicants for jobs that pay far less than would comparable jobs in industry. But in other ways the situation is problematic. Talented people will generally work for inadequate pay for only so long. Eventually, they are lured by other opportunities offering new challenges and more money. While the nonprofit organization is usually able to find young, enthusiastic people to fill the places of departing staff, retaining the experienced employee is more difficult.

Nonprofit organizations are notorious for practicing false economy when it comes to staff salaries. For example, they will hire two incompetent secretaries for more than it would cost to hire one that has good clerical skills and training, would do far better work, and could supervise a couple of volunteers or work-study students for routine filing, typing, and errand running. Or, they set the executive director's salary so low that they cannot attract someone with the kind of credentials and experience necessary to raise money and make the rest of the staff productive. An organization that pays its executive director $50,000 may be able to attract someone who can raise substantial sums of money while a $25,000 executive director may be unable to raise anything. The differential in salary may be significantly less than the difference between what the two can raise.

High salaries are controversial in nonprofit organizations, but they may be necessary to attract top-flight people. One device that some organizations use in order to justify the cost of expensive employees is to "contract" them out to other institutions on a time-available basis at a cost that earns substantial dollars for the organization. The employees must be willing, of course, and the employer should be careful that the necessary organizational work does get done at home. An example of how this works follows.

> The executive director of the Compton Hospital is an expert in the use of computers in hospital administration. His total annual compensation (salary plus benefits) is $44,000. Taking into account holidays, weekends, vacation days, and so on, the actual number of working days per year is 220, thus the director "costs" the hospital $200 per day. Yet it turns out that other organizations are willing to pay $500 per day for the director to come consult with them about computer use in hospital administration. The director, with the permission of the trustees, does some of this consulting on his own time (vacations and weekends), but he has agreed to let the hospital "contract" him out for ten days a year at a rate of $500/day. The hospital takes in $5,000 for these ten "release" days and ends up paying only $39,000 of the $44,000 compensation package from its own coffers.

How much to pay?   The setting of compensation levels is a difficult task, yet there are certain things an organization can do to make it easier. The first is to find as many similar organizations as it is practical to survey, then to call or write them seeking information on employee compensation as well as the type and cost of benefits provided. This information should be summarized for the board showing the lowest, highest, and average salary level for each staff position, together with the range of offered benefits.

Next, the organization's budget should be studied for answers to the following questions: How much can realistically be expended on personnel? How much is necessary for nonpersonnel-related administrative costs (rent, telephone, postage, office supplies, and so on)? Is there enough left over for the organization to carry out its programs and activities? If not, should the staff structure be reworked? Can some work be done by volunteers? by consultants? by work-study students? by other organizations? Can more money be raised? All of these questions may lead to difficult choices. There will probably not be enough money to pay people what they "ought" to be earning. Yet, compensation levels can determine the kind of people who will ultimately decide to work for the organization.

Before any final decisions are made, consideration must be given to whether the organization needs an especially qualified and talented person for a particular job. If a good fund raiser is a priority, the trustees may decide to favor a high salary in the development area. If someone with computer experience is necessary and there is a shortage of data-processing professionals, it may be necessary to bring the salary of this individual up to a level more closely comparable to the level in the profit sector.

Once salary and benefits discussions have been completed, the trustees must set a salary range for each class of positions—executive director, assistant directors, program directors, coordinators, program assistants, clerical/secretarial, and so on. The top dollar figure in a range should be 15 percent to 30 percent higher than the bottom figure. If someone with relatively little experience is offered a job, he or she will probably be offered a compensation level near the bottom of the range but will be able to receive annual merit increases with more experience. Someone coming to the job with plenty of credentials and lots of experience will be offered a salary at a level nearer the top of the range.

Benefits: Today it is not uncommon for prospective employees to look as carefully at benefits packages offered by nonprofit organizations as at salary ranges. This is not surprising. With medical costs rising at a rate far higher than the inflation rate and with inflation itself making retirement seem more like a curse than a blessing, people want to know what the employer can do to assist in these areas. Individual medical plans are expensive so prospective employees will want to know whether there is a group plan available through the employer. There will be questions about disability insurance, life insurance, and tax sheltered annuity plans. More prosaic benefits such as paid holidays, personal days, sick days, paid vacation, and so on will also need to be decided upon by the board and documented for the employees.

In determining benefits, the first thing the trustees must do is to set a target percentage-of-total-salaries figure on which to base the benefits package. For example, suppose the organization says that an amount equal to 13 percent of the total annual payroll will be paid to the employees in the form of benefits. With that figure as a target, they can then determine which combination of benefits is best and how they should be allocated. In budgeting benefits, it is important to leave some unallocated dollars for such employee-related expenses as Workman's Compensation and State Unemployment Insurance, which are technically not considered part of the benefits package. Again, surveying other organizations is useful in attempting to come up with the best combination of benefits. Keep in mind, though, that nonprofit organizations have been slow to introduce adequate benefits packages and newer organizations may want to err on the side of generosity in this area.

Gaining expertise about benefits options available can be accomplished by consulting other organizations, talking to independent insurance agents, discussing the subject with the organization's auditor, and looking to expertise available on the board of trustees. Because of the complexity of the subject and the plethora of choices, it may be desirable to recruit a trustee with experience in this area. This same trustee might also chair a personnel committee, if the board decides to have one.

SETTING POLICIES AND PROCEDURES

After an organization has set the five basic parameters for personnel just discussed, the most important work is done. However, it is desirable to establish additional policies and procedures as follows.

1. Employment and pay procedures
2. Staff evaluation procedures
3. Conflict-of-interest policies
4. Termination and grievance procedures
5. General office practices and procedures

The clearer the policies in each of these areas, the less chance there is for misunderstandings. In addition, organizations that have documented policies in each of these areas are more favorably regarded by government enforcing agencies, prospective trustees, employees, and funders.

EMPLOYMENT AND PAY PROCEDURES

Most employees are interested in knowing as much as they can about an organization's hiring policy. How are employees hired? Is there a formal process with public notice required? Are current employees given first preference for a job? Is there an affirmative action policy? Is hiring done solely on the basis of competence and qualifications? Is every prospective employee allowed to see a job description? There is also interest in the question of what happens to an employee once he or she is hired. Is there an official probationary period? Do temporary or permanent part-time employees enjoy the same rights and benefits as full-time employees? How often are salary ranges and job classifications reviewed and by whom? Another series of questions focuses on pay procedures. How often and in what form are employees paid? What deductions are made from gross wages? What opportunity is there for merit raises? Are there annual cost-of-living increases? Is extra pay available for overtime or extra work?

There are no "right" answers to these questions, but they do provide a kind of checklist of items that the board may wish to discuss and resolve. There are always a number of options and points of view. On the question of promotion-from-within, for example, organizational loyalty tends to be developed when employees view advancement as the reward for good work. Thus, promotion-from-within can be a goal that the board and executive director decide to make into an explicit policy. On the other hand, fresh vision by top management may suggest that, in the case of the executive director's position and positions of senior staff, that outsiders be given preference. Documenting each and every policy once it is decided upon is important. If the organization is vigorously attempting to attract minorities and other special constituencies on to the staff, for example, it is important to state this and have a clearly written affirmative action policy. The morale of employees can be badly bruised when such practices and preferences of the board are not made explicit. Many organizations find probationary periods for new employees useful. During this period the organization or the employee can sever an untenable working relationship without having to resort to the more cumbersome termination or resignation procedures that have been developed for regular employees.

STAFF EVALUATION PROCEDURES

A prospective employee should be made aware of the process by which his or her performance will be evaluated, by whom, how often, and whether salary increases depend on a formal review process. In many organizations, an employee's supervisor meets with the employee once a year for a formal evaluation (the executive director's review, described in Chapter 2, is conducted by the president of the board). A series of questions relating to the job description, performance, employee satisfaction, supervisor satisfaction, and so on can be drawn up. For example:

- Which aspects of your job do you consider to be of highest priority? lowest priority?
- Are there tasks that you are having to perform that are not in your job description? If so, do you feel they should be added or given to someone else?
- Are the demands on your time reasonable?
- Have there been aspects of your job that you have had to neglect for lack of time?
- How well do you feel you are getting along with your co-workers?
- What suggestions do you have about how you could be more productive?
- Do you get enough supervision? too much?
- Is this the right job for you? Which areas are most appealing? Which are least appealing?
- What aspects of your job have you completed most successfully in the last six months? least successfully?
- What do you hope to accomplish in the next six months in your job?
- General comments, complaints, observations, questions.

In addition to asking these questions, the supervisor gives his or her impressions of the strengths and weaknesses of the employee's performance and mentions possible job objectives for the coming year.

After the meeting, the employee writes a summary of the meeting that is submitted to the supervisor. Specific job objectives, agreed upon by both employee and supervisor, are listed. The supervisor reviews the document, adds his or her additional comments, and both sign it. The executive director reviews the document and may decide to intervene if a problem seems to be brewing. Otherwise, the document becomes the basis for a decision regarding a merit increase in salary and ultimately becomes a part of the organization's personnel records.

CONFLICT-OF-INTEREST POLICIES

If employees or trustees of a nonprofit organization are involved in a decision that could result in some sort of financial or other kind of benefit to them or to members of their immediate family, there can be an appearance that the decision was not arrived at objectively, that there was *conflict-of-interest*. Because nonprofit organizations are so clearly mandated to have a broad public purpose and not to serve the parochial interests of board and staff, conflict-of-interest can have particularly negative connotations. For that reason, conflict-of-interest policies should be developed that state clearly how the organization will handle such sensitive situations.

The key to sound policies in this area is what is called *disclosure*. This is because it is not always inappropriate for people to be involved in decisions that may benefit them or a member of their family so long as the nature of the situation is clear to everyone else voting on the matter. Consider, for example, Mary Clarke of the Compton Community Center hiring her husband's law firm to do legal work for the organization. The firm is going to charge far less than its competitors and no one questions the propriety of the decision. Nevertheless, it is important for Mary Clark to "disclose" the nature of the relationship before the board votes on the matter. Thus, conflict-of-interest policies do not necessarily prevent a financial transaction or any other kind of action from taking place, but they do assure an objective review and decision on the issue based on a disclosure of all the facts.

There are times when a "conflict" situation can have a blatant appearance of self-interest. Suppose an organization had to decide whether to buy a piece of property from a family that had three individuals acting as trustees. In this situation, conflict-of-interest policy should prevent these individuals from participating either in the discussion or vote by the board. Because conflict-of-interest situations can be so different from one another and because the appropriate response to them varies, it is advantageous to secure the help of an attorney in drafting appropriate conflict-of-interest policies.

TERMINATION AND GRIEVANCE PROCEDURES

Almost every organization is beset at one time or another with an employee who simply does not work out. As unpleasant as it is to ask someone to leave, sometimes it is necessary for the good of the organization, the other employees, and the individual in question. By the same token, in any hierarchical organization, employees are somewhat at the mercy of their supervisors and there must be organizational safeguards to protect them.

There are some offenses an employee may commit that are grounds for immediate dismissal. These include: falsification of information given for personnel records, drug use during working hours, indecent behavior, theft, pretending illness to avoid work, or gross insubordination. In most cases where a supervisor is unhappy with an employee's performance, however, the situation requires a more moderate response. It is generally a good idea for the two to have a preliminary meeting to discuss the problem. A written record of the meeting should be prepared, signed by both parties, and placed in the personnel file of the employee. The document should summarize the nature of the supervisor's criticism, the employee's response, and the specific job objectives and performance criteria to be used to evaluate that employee's performance in the future. A date should also be set for another meeting to review the employee's progress in the job. In cases where the performance of the employee is so poor that the supervisor thinks termination is a real possibility, the period between the first meeting and the second should be called *probationary* with the understanding that if performance does not improve, the employee will be asked to resign or be fired.

If an employee has a grievance regarding treatment, working conditions, or other matters, the complaint is usually taken up first with that employee's supervisor. If after an initial meeting, or series of meetings, the employee feels that the matter is not satisfactorily resolved, the employee can request a meeting with the person to whom his or her supervisor reports. (This meeting may or may not be with all three present.) In the case where the employee's complaint is with the executive director, the complaint is referred to the chairman of the personnel committee of the board or the board president. In all cases, it is the third individual consulted, the one with the highest position in the organization, who serves as the final arbiter of the problem.

Once an organization sets its policies on warnings, grievances, dismissals, and so on, it is bound by them. A supervisor cannot simply fire an employee without cause if a termination procedure has been established. Employees have legal recourse if the organization's own guidelines are not followed. For this reason, it is often preferable to entice an employee into resigning rather than begin what can be a long and unpleasant process leading to termination. A generous "severance" payment may be all that is required and the "resignation" (which should be made in writing) prevents the employee from claiming unemployment insurance which, at the very least, would lead to higher premium payments.

GENERAL OFFICE PRACTICES AND PROCEDURES

There are a host of little details relating to day-to-day work life that should be spelled out for employees. Some relate specifically to in-office procedures; some are more general. For example, there may be specific rules about how the staff is authorized to make purchases (through purchase orders or petty cash or on a cash reimbursable basis), or there may be specific guidelines governing travel (such as per diem limits, times when air travel is permitted, mileage reimbursement rates, and so on). There may be procedures regulating long distance telephone calls and rules governing the use and care of office equipment. There may be specific limits placed on the organization's liability for personal property left on the premises. In addition, there may be specific guidelines governing outside work, such as whether the employer has first refusal on publications, and whether the organization permits leaves of absence to do outside jobs. Finally, the organization may wish to set policies regarding working hours and conditions that address regular office working hours, "flextime" or "overtime" arrangements,[5] and overtime compensation.

THE PERSONNEL MANUAL

Once all the organizational parameters and specific policies and procedures have been set and voted upon by the board of trustees, they should be collected in one place—put between two covers as it were—and made available to current and prospective employees. A personnel manual is an essential document for any nonprofit organization that has more than

---

[5]When an employee works according to a *flextime* schedule, he or she *substitutes* one set of working hours for another but works the same number of total hours. If the employee works *overtime*, he or she works additional hours beyond the number originally required.

seven or eight employees or a budget in excess of $150,000. (Many smaller organizations have personnel manuals as well.) A typical personnel manual table of contents might look something like this.

PERSONNEL POLICIES, PROCEDURES, AND BENEFITS

Foreword—A brief description of the organization, its philosophy, purposes, and programs

Employment
  Basic Policies
  Hiring Procedures
  Interim (Probationary) period
  Types of Employment (Full-time, Part-time, Temporary)
  Maintenance of Personnel Records

Working Hours and Conditions
  Office Hours
  Flexible Time
  Overtime/Compensatory Time
  Absence Reports

Salaries and Wages
  Salary Structure Through Job Classification
  Paydays
  Deductions
  Raises (Merit and Cost-of-Living)

Employee Benefits
  Leaves and Absences
    Vacations
    Holidays
    Sick Days
    Personal Days
    Maternity Leave
    Paternity Leave
    Leave of Absence
    Other Excused Absences
  Insurance
    Social Security
    Medical Insurance
    Life Insurance
    Disability Insurance
    Unemployment Insurance
    Workman's Compensation

General Policies and Procedures
  Outside Work
  Promotions
  Office Closing
  Telephone
  Travel
  Personal Property

General Office Practices and Procedures
  Office Coverage
  Smoking
  Use and Care of Equipment

Performance and Salary Review
  Timing
  Procedure
  Considerations

Problems
  Grievances
  Suggestions
  Warnings

Termination
  Resignation
  Retirement
  Release
  Discharge
  Final Pay

Organization Chart

Salary Ranges by Position

Conflict of Interest Policies

Personnel Evaluation and Review Procedure

Note: Job descriptions are generally not included in the personnel manual.

Personnel manuals are only useful if they are kept up-to-date. Like job descriptions, they should be reviewed at least annually by the executive director (with help from a trustee, if appropriate). A good clear personnel manual contributes to positive staff morale and prevents the kind of procedural ambiguity that often leads to problems. By comparing personnel manuals from well-managed nonprofits, an organization can distill those elements it considers most important before putting together its own.

SUMMARY

Nonprofit organizations can be very special places to work; similarly it is often the case that their employees are especially committed people. Many could earn more money in other kinds of organizations, but they may be attracted to the nonprofit because of what it contributes to the quality of people's lives.

For this reason, it is important for the trustees to state explicitly in the personnel manual that it regards its employees as one of its most valuable assets. This attitude should also be demonstrated by the interest and compassion that the trustees show toward the staff. It is the trustees's responsibility to set policies that contribute to a harmonious and productive work environment. It is also the trustees's responsibility to praise work that is well done and reward employees who give generously of themselves. Clear and fair personnel policies themselves are only a part of the organization's obligation to the employees. The other part is a positive and caring attitude that reflects the respect and admiration that the employees have earned. In nonprofit organizations particularly, this latter obligation must never be forgotten.

4
Planning

In the 1950s, in an imaginary part of the United States, two mousetrap companies enjoyed halcyon days. Business was good—sales were strong, profit margins were large, employees were happy. While the two companies vied for the title of "Number 1" in the mousetrap manufacturing business, demand for the product was so strong that the competition was friendly. The two companies manufactured quality mousetraps that were hardly distinguishable from one another except for the company labels: The traps had a wooden base, and the spring action mechanism connected to it was of high grade copper wire. Indeed, the very names of the two companies—Better Mousetraps, Inc. and The Superior Trap Company—gave an accurate indication to the world at large that the products being manufactured were "top-of-the-line."

While the products manufactured by these companies were similar, their respective styles of management were very different. Better Mousetraps Inc. (BMI) was a fourth-generation family business. Its president prided himself in running the company the way his father, grandfather, and great grandfather had. "We make the same product the same way we always have," he used to boast, "and I have no doubt that four generations of our customers have used our product with complete satisfaction." The president of Superior Trap Company (STC), a relative new-comer to the industry, was a business school graduate who was constantly involved in product and marketing research as well as in various kinds of business planning. While BMI's president took larger and larger profits out of his company, STC's president used some of his company's earnings to fund a planning division that experimented with alternative materials in the manufacture of traps, considered other uses for their products, and assessed possible changes in consumer demand.

In the 1970s, both companies experienced some serious reversals brought on by greatly increased costs for materials and a decreased demand for mousetraps. The most rapid change affecting the two companies was in the price of copper which doubled in a period of less than 18 months. More mysterious and more gradual was the unexpected drop in consumer demand. Mousetraps simply were not selling as well as they had in the 1950s in spite of the increase in the general population. This seemingly unexplainable shift in demand was a result of the oil crisis of the early 1970s. Because the price of oil had shot up so rapidly and gasoline was in short supply, many people were travelling less and staying home more. The increased hours at home were so lonely that a large number of these people decided to keep pets. The majority of the pets were cats, and because cats perform the same services in the mouse elimination business as traps do, the need for mousetraps decreased.

For BMI, the double reversal of increased cost and decreased demand spelled disaster. The president, who had done everything the way three generations of his family had done it, was convinced that bad times would pass and that persistence, hard work, and tradition would pay off. He was wrong. In 1981, BMI declared bankruptcy. For STC, the situation was quite different. When the price of copper increased, the company substituted a scented shiny steel wire, claiming, as it did so, that ten years of product research had proven that the new trap was 22 percent more effective than the old one. For the next five years, STC captured a larger and larger share of the trap market, thereby further exacerbating BMI's problems. But STC's president knew that this was only a temporary solution, and that indeed, the trap business was doomed by changes in consumer habits and living patterns.

In 1977, STC created a wholly-owned subsidiary, SuTraComp. The name, which was a kind of "high tech" sounding acronym for "Superior Trap/Computer," was appropriate given the product the company became best known for. That product was a high quality computer printout clip—a clip that looked remarkably like the mousetrap the parent company was manufacturing except that its wooden base was decorated not with the head of a mouse, but with a pictorial rendition of a computer terminal and printer spewing forth reams of paper that were gathered up in a compclip (as the product was called). STC spent the next three years marketing the compclip. Ten years of research and planning had indicated that the compclip would be a tremendous seller and, thanks to the company's patent, would be without serious competition.

In the same year that BMI declared bankruptcy, STC discontinued its manufacture of mousetraps. Or, perhaps it would be more accurate to say that STC discontinued *calling* its product a mousetrap. The compclip was now selling so well, that STC's president bought up the remnants of the BMI business and hired the former employees to manufacture the "deluxe compclip," as the copper wire mousetrap was now called. That same year, STC went public and gained a listing on the American Stock Exchange; its president turned down the top job at ailing General Motors. That was also the year that he managed to pay back all of his outstanding loans to business school.

The preceding apocryphal story illustrates the importance of planning. Two companies, both with identical products and markets, ended up at very different points principally because one was willing to allocate resources to long-range planning and the other was not. The successful company (STC) was willing to forego some of its profits in order to underwrite the cost of a planning team; the less successful company (BMI) was not. STC's planners evaluated the company's current operations, charted long-range trends in the marketplace, and considered the ramifications of a variety of alternative scenarios; BMI did none of these things. Although BMI appeared to be more profitable than STC in the 1950s, the failure to allocate some of its resources to planning proved very costly in the end. The company's president learned too late that planning is not a luxury, it is a necessity.

PLANNING FOR NONPROFIT ORGANIZATIONS

In the environment of the profit sector, planning is fairly straightforward. This is because the mission of profit-making companies is clear: They are supposed to make money. In the nonprofit world, where the missions of organizations revolve around the more nebulous concept of *public service,* planning is less straightforward. The reason for this is obvious. Profit is an easy thing to measure; public service is not. A planner can devise and evaluate a number of strategies for making more money and can measure the relative effectiveness of each through quantitative tests. But when the same planner attempts to devise alternative strategies for a nonprofit organization, he or she may discover that the governing group does not even agree on the central mission of the organization. While all agree that the organization is supposed to serve the public, the form of this service is a bit different in each person's mind. For example, a hospital may define its central mission as providing quality health care to the public, but each member of the board and staff may interpret that mission a little differently. One person may believe that the emphasis should be on quality care (top-flight doctors, up-to-date equipment, a university affiliation), while another may believe that service to the public mandates health care for a very broad group of clients, including the indigent and others who cannot or will not pay.

If the lack of agreement over mission is one problem in planning for nonprofit organizations, disagreements about strategies to accomplish the mission is another. Suppose the board and staff can reach a consensus about an organization's mission, now they must debate the best strategy for carrying out that mission. Should a senior citizen service organization provide information or referrals to its clients or should it run programs such as "Meals on Wheels" or recreational activities? Should a multi-racial, multi-ethnic Day Care Center support itself through government contracts or by a sliding scale tuition? Should a food co-op fulfill its mandate of political activism by making contributions to political candidates or boycotting the purchase of lettuce and grapes harvested by nonunion workers? Because the missions of the respective nonprofit organizations are general at best and ambiguous at worst, the strategies for accomplishing them are not clearcut.

Finally, as if the problem over missions and strategies were not enough, there is an additional problem in determining success criteria and evaluation strategies in nonprofit organizations. How does such an organization know whether it is doing a good job in carrying out its mission and accomplishing its goals? For the profit-making company, the measurement of success is relatively simple. It is accomplished through an examination of the financial balance sheet. A series of numbers shows whether the company is succeeding and compares its current performance with performance in other years. Unfortunately, in the nonprofit world, success is not only more difficult to measure but it is even difficult to define. One trustee of a community theater might argue that the cost-effectiveness of the organization's inner-city program is an appropriate measure of its success; another may feel that the proper criterion is the number of clients served; still another may argue that success should be judged by the critical response to the program by the media.

With so much disagreement over mission, strategies, and success criteria, it is no wonder that many nonprofit organizations resist planning. The reasons for not planning are varied. For example, planning takes too much time and effort (the staff is already overworked and the board does not even have enough time to discuss present crises), or planning is too expensive (there is no extra money in the budget for consultants, the costs of meetings, and other expenses). One of the most popular arguments that nonprofits use to justify not planning is that "we must remain open and responsive to our constituents so we shouldn't let ourselves be trapped by a long-range plan."

Not one of these arguments is justified. To argue that staff and board do not have enough time to do planning is a bit like arguing that the fiscal officer does not have time to prepare a budget and the treasurer does not have time to review it. Because these tasks are a part of their job responsibilities, they must make time. To argue that there is no money in the budget to pay for planning is like saying that there is nothing in the budget for rent and utilities. If the money is not there, it should be put there. To argue that an organization should be responsive to its constituency is an argument for planning, not against it because planning involves an analysis of the needs of the constituency both in the present and in the future.

There is only one justifiable argument against planning. When planning is done badly, it is not only a waste of time but it also saps the energies and the spirit of an organization's board, staff, and sometimes even its constituency. Long, laborious, expensive planning processes that result in voluminous documents no one reads are an argument against planning. Yet, planning is so important, and its absence leaves an organization so vulnerable, that it is worthwhile to attempt to find a planning process that can work, which is the subject of the balance of this chapter.

WHAT IS A PLANNING PROCESS?

Planning is an ongoing process involving several steps that are listed below.

> Step 1—Set parameters and boundaries.
> Step 2—Identify limiting conditions.
> Step 3—Change limiting conditions where possible.
> Step 4—Design a plan of action.
> Step 5—Carry out the action plan.
> Step 6—Evaluate what you have done.
> Step 7—Repeat the whole process.

PLANNING A GARDEN

In order to gain a better understanding of what each step involves, imagine that you are a gardener and that you have been given the task of taking a plot of land, turning it into a garden, and maintaining that garden year after year. If you went through the seven steps, you would do the following things.

Set parameters and boundaries: First, you would determine the boundaries of your garden, taking into account your property lines, the general contour of the land, how much you wanted to produce in the garden, and how hard you were willing to work. You would make your decisions with care, thinking about the long-term future of this garden. After all, once you decided on the boundaries, prepared the ground, built fences, and put in the surrounding trees and lawn, you would be reluctant to go through the time, expense, and stress that would be required to make a change.

Identify limiting conditions: Second, you would identify conditions that determined what you could plant in your garden. Climate would be the first limiting factor: when does the ground freeze and thaw? how much rainfall is there and how long are the dry periods? how many hours of daylight and how much direct sun will different parts of the garden receive? A second factor would be soil conditions: is the soil acidic or alkaline? sandy or clay? does it have adequate organic nutrients? A third constraint would involve your budget: how much money are you willing to spend on the garden? how much help are you likely to get (both in manpower and dollars) to stretch the resources that you have?

Change limiting conditions where possible: Third, you would now see if there were ways to change some of the limiting conditions you had identified in the previous step. For example, if you had determined that the ground stayed frozen until late March, yet you knew you wanted to start some of your vegetables well before that time, you might consider investing in a greenhouse or a coldframe, or you might decide to buy seedlings instead of seeds. If you discovered that an oak tree shaded half of the garden for three hours in the afternoon, you might decide to cut it down or at least remove some of its limbs. If you found out that your soil was poor, you would seriously consider adding fertilizer. But how much money would you be willing to spend in preparing the soil and making some of these other changes? Remember, your limited budget has to cover these "modifications" plus the cost of the garden itself. Or does it? Is your budget really inelastic or is this another limitation that you may be able to modify?

Design a plan of action: Fourth, you are now ready to plan the specific actions you will take. In essence, you are ready to lay out the garden. You will decide how to prepare the ground, what seeds and plants to buy, whether to do some preplanting in a greenhouse or cold frame, when you need outside help, when to harvest the produce, what you must do to "winterize" the garden and protect certain plants from harsh weather after the first growing season, and on and on. Unfortunately, there are many gardeners (even experienced ones) who start the planning process at this point. While they may have excellent gardens, the gardens themselves tend to look the same year after year. The boundaries have been established years before and there has never been any thought about changing them. The gardeners have learned, often by trial and error, what grows and what does not, so they tend to plant the same thing in the same place year in and year out. But despite the fact that their gardens look nice, these gardeners are creatures of habit. This can be a problem if changes occur over which they have little or no control (a sudden shrinking of budget, acid rain, a need to expand the boundaries of the garden). These gardeners have few strategies for responding to such change.

Carry out the action plan: Fifth, you are now ready to actually carry out the plan for the garden. If you have done all the preceding steps correctly, your garden should end up looking very nice. There will be some surprises and some disappointments, but for the most part, your garden should look quite acceptable. If it does not, chances are you skimped on your planning because you were so excited about actually starting right in on planting. This, unfortunately, is the plight of most inexperienced gardeners. They actually *begin* by planting their gardens and the results are often unfortunate. Because they have done virtually no planning, they do not know what grows best or what they can do to improve the conditions for growth. They go to a nursery, buy lovely healthy plants only to see these plants wither in the ground two weeks later. They complain that they do not have the proverbial "green thumb" not realizing that green thumbs are not inherited but are earned by good planning and hard work.

Evaluate what you have done: Sixth, if your garden is growing well you are probably more worried about weeds, rodents, and insects than you are about next year's garden. But as you plant, cultivate, and weed, and as you pick your flowers and harvest your vegetables, you must carefully observe your successes and your failures with an eye toward next year's garden. Evaluation is an essential component of good planning because it allows you, the gardener, to test your hypotheses and adjust them in the future based on actual events.

Repeat what you have done: Seventh, it is time to repeat the process for next year. Actually, the process is a bit different the second time around. As you were planning your first garden, you spent a great deal of time on step 1 determining the shape, contours, and boundaries of the garden. During the second year, it is unlikely that you will spend nearly as much time (if any) thinking about this. However, you will find it important periodically to review step 1. As your resources increase, you may become more ambitious and want to add a rock garden where you originally thought gardening was out of the question; as you grow older, you may want to shrink the boundaries of your garden so that you can still manage things without too much strain. Whatever you decide, you want to do it with adequate thought and deliberation, not just on impulse.

There is one other observation to make about your garden planning. Although a sequence of steps has been given, it is quite possible that a skilled gardener may be working on several steps at the same time and may be planning for several different years at once. For example, a gardener may be thinking now about changing the boundaries of his garden five years hence. At the same time, he or she may be planning the ramifications this will have on budget, soil preparation, and coldframe construction over the next three years while planning the specific layout of this year's garden. A skilled planner knows that planning is an ongoing process in which many things interact simultaneously.

PLANNING IN A NONPROFIT ORGANIZATION

In a nonprofit organization, each of the steps just described must take place in a planning process. When the organization is first set up, the broad parameters of its activities must be established. They are generally documented in a mission statement that is contained in the Articles of Organization. Periodically, this mission statement should be reviewed so that trustees can make sure the organization is still operating within the established boundaries and decide whether the mission statement itself should be changed. Second, a nonprofit organization must look at those factors that constrain its activities—budgetary considerations, government regulations, the wishes of its constituency and/or membership, societal trends—to understand what limitations must be taken into account in planning. Third, it must decide which of those constraints can be modified or changed and which are worth changing. For example, additional fund raising might eliminate some budget constraints; a public relations or education campaign for the membership might change its views on certain issues; political activism might lead to changes in certain government regulations. Fourth, the organization must map out a specific action plan for the immediate future, including the approval of a budget (which makes priorities clear) and a program plan. Fifth, the plan must be carried out. Sixth, activities must be evaluated in order to help future planning. Finally, the whole process must be repeated.

LEVELS OF PLANNING

One way to think about planning is to view it sequentially as a series of steps as we have just done. The problem with a description of a sequential process is that it can be somewhat misleading because a group of planners will probably not wait for one step to be completed before beginning on another. In fact, several planning steps may be taking place at the same time. For that reason, it is probably more useful to talk about *levels* of planning as follows.

1. The level of purpose or mission
2. The level of goals
3. The level of objectives/targets

4. The level of strategies
5. The level of actions
6. The level of evaluation

Planning levels relate closely (but not precisely) to the planning steps described in the previous section. Let us look at this more carefully. Suppose you are planning a trip:

— *Purpose* reveals why you are going.
— *Goals* tells what direction you are going to head.
— *Objectives/targets* reveal your specific destination.
— *Strategies* tell how you will get there.
— *Actions* are the trip itself.
— *Evaluation* determines whether you arrived.

How can these planning levels be translated into a planning process for a nonprofit organization? The question can be answered by looking at planning within a specific nonprofit organization, the Compton Memorial Hospital. The mission of the hospital was set out at its inception and is reviewed periodically and, occasionally, even amended. A mission statement tells the world why the organization exists and what general categories of activities are within its purview. The *mission* of the Compton Memorial Hospital is "to provide quality health care to the people of Compton." At first glance, it would appear that such a mission statement would never have to be revised. After all, providing quality health care is what a hospital is all about. Yet, it is quite possible that 50 years hence a new, more modern hospital may be established in Compton. At that point, Compton Memorial must decide whether it wants to compete (with its outdated plant and equipment), wants to go out of business, or wants to change its mission (it might become an out-patient facility). At that point, its governing group must examine the mission statement and determine the nature and scope of changes that need to be made.

At the second planning level, the level of *goals*, a more specific series of statements must be developed setting the direction of the organization's activities for the shorter term. Thus, while the Compton Memorial Hospital's mission is "to provide quality health care to the people of Compton," its specific goals for the next five years might be: to establish an out-patient unit; to improve administrative practices, particularly in the areas of record keeping and billing; to pursue collaborative planning of health care delivery with surrounding hospitals; and to establish greater financial stability through increased fund raising. Though goal statements are more specific than a mission statement in setting a direction for the organization, they do not state exactly what the organization is going to do, how it is going to do it, and what the criteria will be to determine success. What goal statements do provide is the framework for deciding these more specific questions.

It is at the third planning level, the level of *objectives/targets*, that the goals are interpreted, made more specific, and quantified. An objective is a specific "destination" statement. It describes very specifically where an organization wishes to go. Every objective carries with it either a stated or implied target, a measurable benchmark that determines whether the organization achieved the objective. Thus, goals give a general indication of direction, objectives indicate the destination, and targets offer criteria for judging whether the destination was reached. For example, one of the hospital's goals is "to improve administrative practices, particularly in the area of record keeping and billing." The problem with that statement by itself is that it is too general. No one knows what *specific* things need to be achieved in order to carry out the goal successfully. Therefore, an objective/target must be developed. An example might be to have the entire billing system computerized within two years. If another goal of the hospital is to establish greater financial stability through increased fund raising, an objective/target might be to increase private donations by 10 percent a year for three years. At this point, great care must be taken to set realistic targets because it is by these targets that the board and staff will evaluate their success. In the case of the computerized billing system, staff members may appear incompetent if they agree to an unrealistic timetable; in the case of the increased fund-raising target, board members should be confident that they have the time and are willing to make the commitment that such an optimistic target suggests. In the end, success is judged not by the optimism of the original objective but by whether the target was achieved.

The fourth level of planning involves *strategies* for carrying out the objectives and reaching the targets. Strategies are also called *action plans*. If objectives tell us where we want to get, strategies and action plans tell us how we are going to get there and how much it will cost. (A complete action plan includes a detailed budget for each suggested strategy.) Because action plans assign specific costs to particular objectives, they are generally worked up by staff and fully discussed by the board before a set of objectives/targets is approved. For example, the board of the Compton Memorial Hospital did not agree to increase private donations by 10 percent a year for three years until the staff had come up with an action plan to show how this could be accomplished and how much it would cost. The action plan budgeted for a fund-raising consultant during the first six months of the campaign; called for additional volunteers (to be recruited by a board committee) to work on an annual telethon; mandated another board committee to organize an annual auction beginning in the second year; and suggested the need for a senior level staff person (with clerical assistance) to coordinate the campaign. These strategies represented only a small part of the staff's total action plan for this objective.

The fifth level of planning is implementation of the *action plan* itself. Very little actual planning goes on at this level as this is more of a *doing* phase. However, careful monitoring must take place to be sure that the implementation is proceeding on schedule. For example, the Compton Memorial Hospital assigned two board members to develop a volunteer list for the telethon. After two months, nothing had been done (one board member had had a death in the family and the other was simply overwhelmed by the task). For that reason, modifications were made in the action plan—four board members were asked to find volunteers, and a staff person was assigned to assist this group on a half-day-a-week basis.

The sixth and final level of planning is *evaluation*. Evaluation asks the questions: did we achieve our targets? why or why not? how can we do better next time? Evaluation is an extremely important planning tool because it provides concrete information on the organization's performance potential based on past experience. As a result, it makes future planning easier and more realistic. For example, when the board of the Compton Memorial Hospital examined the performance of its fund-raising drive after three years, it found that private donations had not increased significantly for the first 18 months of the campaign but thereafter increased 35 percent in a six-month period. The evaluator's conclusion was that it takes several months to set up a good fund-raising campaign and that the board should not have expected concrete results immediately. This fact was extremely useful to the board as it planned its fund-raising target for the next three years. The target called for a 30 percent increase over a three-year period with the increases phased annually at 5 percent, 10 percent, and 15 percent.

PLANNING LEVEL RESPONSIBILITIES

One of the advantages of looking at planning in terms of levels is that it can be a more useful framework for determining who is responsible for what in the planning process itself. For example:

1. The board of directors is responsible for mission statements.
2. The board, with the assistance of staff, is responsible for setting goals.
3. Board and staff are jointly responsible for setting objectives/targets.

4. Staff, with the approval of board, is responsible for determining strategies.
5. Staff is responsible for implementing the action plan.
6. Board and staff are responsible for approving an evaluation plan. Ideally it should be carried out by an objective outsider.

Once again, it should be stressed that planning is not necessarily a sequential process in which one level always precedes another. Rather, it is usually a dynamic process in which work can be done on several levels at once. The decision concerning the actual sequence of planning activities depends on the planning model used by the organization.

PLANNING MODELS

There are numerous planning models used in nonprofit organizations. It is probably not very important for administrators and board members of nonprofit organizations to become familiar with each and every one of them. What is important is to understand the two underlying approaches to planning, *linear planning* and *integrated planning*, which ultimately dictate what planning model is chosen. Each of these approaches has its own particular advantages and disadvantages. Once these are fully understood, the governing group of a nonprofit organization, together with its senior staff, can develop a specific model of planning that seems appropriate both for the organization and the particular planning situation.

LINEAR PLANNING

Many classical planning models are based on a linear approach. The linear approach assumes that planning for any particular phase of an organization's operation has a beginning point and an end point. The beginning point is usually the process of drafting mission statements or purposes; the end point is the formulation of a very specific action plan. The linear model is very comprehensive and is often used when an organization finds itself taking on planning for the first time or involving itself in a new area of activity. In addition, the linear model is often used when an organization needs to demonstrate wide involvement of the general public in the planning process or has to draft a plan that will become a public document open to review and comment by friends and foes alike.

Linear planning proceeds by a process of condensation and

distillation following the steps outlined earlier in the chapter. It considers a whole range of options at each level of planning (mission, goals, objectives, strategies) and in each case eliminates all but the very few that appear most reasonable and sensible. The linear planning model is best described visually by a triangle.

FIGURE 4.1.

The triangle, a visual metaphor for linear planning over time, reveals two special characteristics of this approach to planning. First, it shows how linear planning always proceeds from a process of broad mission and goal formulation to the more narrow and specific process of writing action plans; and, second, it shows how linear planning tends to slough off many options and narrow down to a very few.

Linear planning has advantages and disadvantages. The principal advantage is its comprehensiveness. When a nonprofit organization undertakes a controversial, risky, or expensive new project, or significantly changes its mission, it can prove to the world at large that the new direction has not been undertaken lightly, that many people have been consulted, and that many options have been considered. A second advantage is that a linear planning process often generates a formal public document that provides the framework for actions and protects the organization from pressures to consider other approaches.

Unfortunately, the very comprehensiveness of linear planning is one of its major disadvantages. It is often a slow and frustrating process. Many organizations spend months drafting mission statements, begin to tackle goals, and simply give up in exhaustion without a plan and without a willingness to continue planning in the future. Inflexibility is a second disadvantage. Once a plan has been drafted and approved, it is very difficult to change. Should conditions change, if opportunities arise, if the plan itself does not seem to be on track, the plan is not easy to modify. Additionally, such a lengthy process often places an organization in a holding pattern that restricts the implementation of new initiatives.

INTEGRATED PLANNING

There are many planning models that do not depend on a predictable sequential process but instead are based on a more integrated approach, an approach in which the various planning components are interdependent with one another. Integrated planning models do not have predictable beginning and end points, nor do they assume that it is necessary to complete one step in the planning process before undertaking another step. Rather, this approach utilizes the concept of "strategic fit," suggesting that the various components of planning must be fit together to make a coherent whole. To accomplish such a fit, every detail in the planning process must be capable of influencing every other. As a result, all components of planning—mission statements, goal formulation, the development of objectives/targets, action plans, and evaluation—must take place constantly so that as information is generated from one area it can influence decisions and choices made in another.

In linear planning, information flow tends to be in one direction. Thus, information about mission determines goal formulation but not the other way around. Goals determine objectives; objectives determine strategies, and so on. In integrated planning, information flows in several directions because every planning component is interdependent and can affect and be affected by any other. An organization's mission is tied inextricably to its actions, to the evaluation of those actions, to available resources that often determine strategies, to the needs of the constituency as defined in many of the goals, and so on. As a result, integrated planning must be informed by various kinds of ongoing information gathering. It is not sufficient to collect information for a particular phase of planning only once. Information must be collected continually as other phases of the planning process redefine the original questions asked.

An integrated planning model is best represented visually by a circle that resembles a wheel with spokes. The planning coordinator or coordinating group sits at the center of the wheel collecting information from and communicating it to the wheel's perimeter via the spokes. At the perimeter, various people are working on specific tasks. These tasks are already familiar to us—one group may be evaluating current activities, another might be reviewing statements of purpose, a third might be surveying the organization's membership to formulate new goals for the future, a fourth might be talking to potential funders and working on budgets leading to a formulation of strategies, a fifth might be proposing specific action plans, and so forth. (In some cases, one group or even one individual might take on several of these tasks). In order for the wheel to turn—representing the organization's forward progress in planning— the planning coordination process must take place at the center. This involves three types of activity: collecting information from the planning groups at the wheel's perimeter, communicating relevant information back to these groups, and ultimately fitting together all the pieces of information into a coherent plan.

FIGURE 4.2.

Integrated planning is by its very nature an ongoing process. Like the wheel that serves as the visual metaphor for the process, it has no beginning point and no end point and is continually moving. For this reason, integrated planning tends to emphasize the *process* of planning. This is one of its advantages over linear planning. Unlike linear planning, an integrated process enables an organization to be responsive to change, to opportunity, and to setbacks. It does not have to "begin the process of planning all over again" in order to respond to a sudden change in the funding environment, political reversals, or changes in staffing and governance that could lead to new opportunities and activities. Rather, when changes occur, mission statements can be reviewed, goals can be reformulated, and action plans can be drafted, all at the same time. It is the role of the planning coordinator (or planning committee) to see that all of these tasks are completed, that there is adequate communication flow, and that the results of the various components of planning dovetail to make a coherent whole.

A second advantage of integrated planning is that it encourages the board, staff, and constituency to remain involved in the process. In linear planning, it is easy to get bogged down at the level of missions and goals. People become tired and discouraged. Because they have only one opportunity to discuss missions and goals, they tend to spend too much time being careful to "get it right." In integrated planning, the process drives itself forward. A discussion of strategies does not wait for the discussion of missions to be "completed" because there is no such thing as closure on that discussion. What does happen is that the planning coordinator/group puts pressure on those discussing mission statements to come up with at least a preliminary draft so that the other parts of the planning process can continue. Because this draft can always be revised as the planning process moves forward, and as the various planning components fit together, no air of finality hangs over the draft passed along.

A third advantage of integrated planning is that it tends to move more quickly toward actions. Linear planning models, as we have seen, are slow because they assume that distillation is the essence of planning and that in any planning decision, every reasonable alternative should be considered. Though this does lead to informed choices in planning, those choices may be a long time in coming. Integrated planning cannot claim to be as comprehensive. What it gives up in comprehensiveness, it gains in time.

The very advantages of integrated planning suggest the disadvantages. Its lack of comprehensiveness can lead to uninformed decisions that result in rash actions; its flexibility can have a negative effect on people's confidence in the organization's long-term plans; and the emphasis on process usually means that a carefully organized, well-documented, written plan is a second priority, one that is often not addressed.

WHICH APPROACH?

Clearly, then, each approach offers advantages and disadvantages for particular kinds of organizations in particular situations. For this reason, an organization must think carefully about planning approaches before it begins to plan and must develop an appropriate model to meet its needs. If an organization is new, has never planned before, is undertaking a controversial activity or one that will take it into uncharted waters, the comprehensiveness of a linear approach may be appropriate. Integrated approaches may be better for day-to-day planning, for ongoing planning work that attempts to involve a broad range of people in setting the best course for the future, and for planning requiring quick decisions and rapid response to change. Every organization should decide on a planning approach not by falling into the familiar but by consciously choosing an approach that seems right for the time, the situation, the people involved (both within and outside the organization), and the organization itself.

THE ROLE OF A PLANNING COMMITTEE

To do effective planning, most organizations find it useful to have a planning committee composed of some trustees, staff members, and, occasionally, people from outside the organization. The role of the planning committee is to collect and organize material that can be presented to the full board for discussion and action. It should operate on an annual schedule that allows the appropriate items to come to the board at the proper time in the fiscal year. In addition, a planning committee should have built-in liaison with other committees so that it can coordinate the planning of each group and organize all of the specific plans into a coherent whole.

A planning committee should always be looking at three different time frames as it goes about its work: the immediate future, the medium-range future, and the long-term future. At each meeting, different emphases should be placed on each of these time frames depending on where the group finds itself in the planning cycle. For example, at one meeting, the planning committee may spend almost no time discussing the organization's long-term future because it must put the finishing touches on the action plan for the upcoming fiscal year. At its next meeting, the discussion may shift almost exclusively to long-term future planning issues. The determining factor will be the needs of the full board. If the trustees must approve a budget for the upcoming fiscal year, they must have all the planning information relative to that year before taking a final vote; if the trustees are discussing and approving a program plan for two years hence, they need a full report on the issues from the planning committee. Thus, the committee's work should be completely integrated with the decision cycle of the board itself.

In some organizations, the cycle of planning committee meetings and board meetings follows a predictable pattern. At each point in the year, the planning responsibilities of both groups is clearly laid out. Consider the following nonprofit foundation whose fiscal year begins on September 1. The schedule and planning content of the board and committee meetings are as follows.

Planning Committee—September meeting
1. Brief discussion of any need for changes in the plan for the fiscal year just begun for board consideration in November.
2. Extensive discussion of the program plan for the fiscal year beginning

one year hence with recommendations to be circulated to full board for action in November.

3. Brief discussion of long-term policy or program issues that should be discussed during the year that will influence planning decisions.

Board of Trustees—November meeting

1. Action on recommended changes in current fiscal year plan.
2. Extensive discussion and preliminary approval of program plan for the year beginning ten months hence. Board instructions to planning committee and staff on areas requiring further research and refinement.
3. Discussion of long-term policy/program issues identified by committee at the September meeting.

Planning Committee—December meeting

1. Brief discussion of need for changes in current fiscal year plan.
2. Brief discussion of further refinements in next year's plan.
3. Extensive discussion of long-term policy and program issues, including those affecting mission, goals, programs, trustees, staff, constituency. (Some of these issues will be scheduled for full board discussion.)

Board of Trustees—January meeting

1. Action on recommended changes in current fiscal year plan.
2. Report on additional material collected for next fiscal year's plan.
3. Extensive discussion and preliminary resolution of long-term policy and program issues selected for full board discussion by planning committee in December.

Planning Committee—March meeting

1. Extensive half-year evaluation of current fiscal year with recommendations to board on changes in budget, programs, and so on as needed.
2. Brief discussion of further refinements in next year's plan.
3. Brief discussion of how the long-term policy and program issues discussed by the board can be built into future plans.

Board of Trustees—April meeting

1. Discussion and approval of changes in current fiscal year plan.
2. Update on further refinements in next year's plan.
3. Update on how long-term policy and program issues are being incorporated into planning process.

Planning Committee—June meeting

1. Extensive discussion of next year's plan including final budget figures. (This plan is to be recommended to the full board for approval.)
2. Preliminary discussion of the plan for the following year (beginning 15 months hence).

3. Further discussion of how the long-term policy issues resolved by the board can be incorporated into the plan for the year beginning 15 months hence.

Board of Trustees—July meeting

1. Final approval of next year's plan, including budget.
2. Preliminary discussion of plan for the year beginning 15 months hence.
3. Report by planning committee on long-term policy issues.

What is interesting in this example is that the planning committee is under constant pressure to produce material for the full board to discuss and act upon. It cannot sit back and have general philosophical discussions unless it completes the very specific assigned tasks. As a result, the meetings of this group must be highly structured and very efficient. Every member of the committee is given an assignment and reports are prepared in advance of meetings for everyone to read and discuss.

At the June meeting of this committee, a transition is made in the planning phases. Between September and June, this committee has regarded the current fiscal year of the organization as the *immediate* future and the following year of the organization as the *medium-range* future. In June, the committee abandons any consideration of the current year. Next year, the fiscal year three months away, thus becomes the *immediate* future concern; and the fiscal year 15 months away becomes the *medium-range* future concern. Thus, the committee is always forcing itself to jump ahead in its thinking and its planning.

The schedule laid out in the previous example is but one way an organization can set up its planning activities for the year. There are other systems that may be equally effective. For example, some organizations may find it more convenient to organize their meetings topically. It is common, for example, for a planning committee to work on mission statements at one meeting, goals and objectives at another, action plans at a third, and so forth. What is crucial is that there be a system to ensure that the committee keeps to a schedule, reports regularly to the board, and that planning continue throughout the year.

While good planning is always a healthy combination of information gathering, discussion, and common sense, many organizations suffer from a "where do we start" syndrome. They simply do not know what information should be collected and how it should be discussed. They have no sense of what the planning "issues" are that need to be resolved. In order to get the board and staff of organizations like these on track, it is sometimes useful to follow a schedule like the one previously outlined that has very clear demands and deadlines.

SUMMARY

For any organization setting up a planning process, the following comments, which conclude the chapter, may be especially useful to keep in mind.

1. The simpler the planning process, the more likely it is to succeed.
2. There is no one "right way" to plan. The best planning processes are those custom designed to fit the needs of an organization and the working styles of board and staff.
3. The primary benefit of planning is usually the process, not the product. Planning is a structured way of involving a number of people in thinking about the future, and this is often its chief value.
4. Planning is not necessarily a synonym for growth. Scaling down activities (or eliminating them) may often be an appropriate planning decision.
5. Planning produces conflict and anxiety. No one can completely control the outcome of a planning process and this produces tensions among board and staff. This feeling is often augmented by frustration over the amount of time required in planning.
6. The desire for consensus almost always impedes the planning process. It is important to hear everyone's views. It is not advantageous to incorporate every minority opinion into a plan.
7. To be successful, a planning process must have the strong support of top-level staff, key trustees, and others of influence in the organization.
8. Planning should not be left to professional planning consultants. Staff and board must be involved so that the decisions reached are their own.
9. Perhaps most important, there must be a climate of enthusiasm within the organization toward planning. Without it, a planning process has little chance of success.

5

Financial Management

Financial management is, for many, one of the most forbidding aspects of the administration of nonprofit organizations. This is because many people come into nonprofit organizations without a financial or administration background. Often they have chosen to work as staff members or serve on boards because of a knowledge and commitment to education, the arts, or some other intrinsically interesting activity. For them, the financial area—budgets, reports, statements, procedures— seems unrelated and dull, something for the "financial" people to deal with. Yet, as we all know, finances cannot be left to financial people. Budgeting is a function of overall organizational planning and the setting of priorities; analyzing financial statements is an important way to take a measure of an organization's health while at the same time protecting the organization's interests and those of the public. Sound internal financial procedures are necessary to stay within the law and to offer acceptable assurances to donors that their monies are safe.

Part of the reason that people become confused with financial management and draw away from it is because financial experts use a special language. There are many terms that serve as shorthand for basic financial concepts. The concepts themselves are not difficult; neither is the language, once you know it. However, many people were never taught what the terms mean and some continue their involvement with nonprofit organizations remaining confused about important financial decisions. This chapter and the one that follows introduce some of the financial terms and explain many of the concepts. It will become clear that financial management is an intrinsically logical, albeit sometimes boring, subject. The concepts may be dull, but for the most part they are not difficult. This chapter deals with aspects of planning for the fiscal year, most especially developing budgets and cash flow projections. The following chapter explains how to keep financial records.

THE FINANCIAL, OR "FISCAL," YEAR

We all make plans and keep records; and we usually have some systematic way of doing so. In financial management, planning and record keeping is set up according to fixed time periods, the most common of which is the fiscal year. Because *fiscal* is simply another word for *financial,* the fiscal year is the financial (or accounting) year of the organization, the period for which all financial transactions are grouped together, added up, and reported upon. For individuals, the fiscal year begins on January 1 and ends on December 31. This is the time period in which individuals group financial transactions for tax purposes. We can say that the fiscal year for individuals is the same as the calendar year (both begin January 1). For nonprofit organizations, however, the fiscal year is not always the same as the calendar year. In fact, a nonprofit corporation can specify any dates for its fiscal year. It simply specifies in its Articles of Organization that "the corporation's fiscal year ends on (date) each year." That date could be the executive director's birthday or the anniversary date of the organization's founding, though neither of these choices is likely to be in the best interests of the organization.

How should a nonprofit organization choose a fiscal year? The following two considerations should be kept in mind.

1. The fiscal year should roughly parallel the organization's program year. That is, one year's program activities should not fall into two fiscal years. If the academic year for a school runs from September to June, for example, it would be unwise to set the fiscal year to run concurrently with the calendar year. The result would be that the academic year would fall into two fiscal years and it would be difficult to prepare budgets and analyze the financial performance of the school on an annual program year basis.

2. The fiscal year should end, whenever possible, just before a period of relative inactivity. There is a great deal of effort involved in closing the books at the end of the fiscal year. If an audit is involved, and in most organizations it is, an accountant needs to check financial records and review bank statements. Since this places a heavy burden on the financial staff, the audit should take place when other demands on staff time are minimal.

It is an unfortunate fact of life that the government and other public and private funding sources require an organization to keep certain records according to their accounting periods. Often these do not correspond to the organization's fiscal year. For example, payroll records must be kept on a calendar year basis in order to satisfy federal and state government accounting needs and to give salaried employees and independent contractors their W-2 and 1099 forms respectively for tax purposes. A particular corporation may stipulate that a final report is due at the end of the calendar year showing how its money was spent during the previous 12-month period.

Obviously, all of this separate record keeping is time-consuming and many organizations are resorting to computers to keep their financial records. Once the information is in a computer, the machine can reorganize it according to any time period requested. With the rapidly decreasing costs of small microcomputers, and the availability of prepackaged software to handle accounting needs, organizations with a heavy volume of financial transactions, especially those requiring the reorganization of records according to differing accounting periods, should seriously consider this option (see Chapter 7). In addition, many organizations hand all of their payroll record keeping over to a specialized payroll accounting service. This service is offered by banks and other financial institutions. It may include the preparation of paychecks, the maintenance of tax and benefit information, the issuing of W-2 and 1099 forms, and other payroll-related tasks. Because these services are fully computerized, they are often less expensive than having comparable tasks done manually by one of the organization's own paid staff members.

THE BUDGET

A budget is a financial plan. It specifies how much money an organization thinks it will take in and how much it will spend. A budget is generally laid out in two sections that are grouped under two main headings: *Income* (or Revenue) and *Expense* (or Expenditure) (see Figure 5.1). Within the two sections, there is a further subdivision into income and expense categories. Each of these categories is placed on its own line with a dollar estimate listed beside it. For this reason, these categories are called "line items." Another name for a line item is an "account." Thus, for example, when someone refers to the "salary account," the reference is to that line item in the budget in which all salary expenditures are grouped. All line items (or accounts) taken together are called the "chart of accounts." This is the listing of all the budget categories.

How does an organization decide what categories to include in its chart of accounts? After all, there are many ways to break down the same financial information. For example, a hospital could decide to

FIGURE 5.1. Single Fund Budget of the Compton School

INCOME		EXPENSES	
Tuition	$41,000	Salaries	$38,200
Book Store Sales	10,000	Benefits	4,000
Foundation Grant	5,000	Honoraria	2,500
Business Scholarships	5,000	Supplies and Materials	5,200
Individuals	23,000	Equipment Rental	3,400
Total	$84,000	Promotion	6,500
		Facility Rental	20,000
		Contingency/Reserve	4,200
		Total	$84,000

lump all salaries under a single line item. Or it could subdivide salaries into many categories such as:

Salaries—physicians
Salaries—nursing staff
Salaries—administrative
Salaries—custodial

Every organization has to decide for itself on an appropriate chart of accounts. It must balance its need for detailed breakdowns of financial projections and records with the need to keep things simple. The best way to develop a chart of accounts is to look at the accounts of similar organizations that are well managed and have been around for some time. Compare the various listings of accounts. Look for commonalities and differences. Take into consideration your own special needs. Then begin to develop your chart of accounts based on the collective wisdom you have gained.

THE SINGLE FUND BUDGET

A small organization may have a single budget for its entire operation—a kind of composite statement of the predicted expense and income for the entire organization. The budget in Figure 5.1 is such a budget and is called a *single fund budget*. As organizations grow more complex, however, they may need to develop several subdivisions of this budget in order to gain a detailed analysis of the operation. For example, suppose an opera company has both a home season and a touring season; it might prove useful to develop separate budgets for each so that the costs of each part of the operation can be analyzed. Obviously, when all the sub-budgets are added together, a total organizational budget (or single fund budget) can be computed.

PROJECT BUDGETING

Project budgeting (see Figure 5.2) allows an organization not only to analyze its various activities, but it allows for greater flexibility in developing budgets for fund-raising purposes. For example, in Figure 5.2, the opera company's touring program shows a deficit while the home season does not. However, the bulk of the revenues from the home season come from ticket sales which are unrestricted as to their use and therefore transferable to any part of the organization's operation. Let us suppose that the director of the "Friendly Foundation" tells the director

FIGURE 5.2. Project Budgeting
Compton Opera Company

BUDGET #1
(Note "deficit" in touring project)

Account	Home Season	Touring	Total
INCOME			
Ticket Sales	$62,500	$ -0-	$ 62,500
Road Fees	-0-	45,000	45,000
National Endowment	-0-	5,000	5,000
State Arts Council	10,000	-0-	10,000
Individuals	5,000	5,000	10,000
TOTAL	$77,500	$55,000	$132,500
EXPENSES			
Salaries	$56,000	$21,500	$ 77,500
Living Allowance	-0-	18,000	18,000
Travel Expenses	-0-	8,000	8,000
Scenery, Etc.	8,000	2,000	10,000
Truck	500	4,500	5,000
Promotion	2,000	2,000	4,000
Administration	11,000	4,000	15,000
TOTAL	$77,500	$60,000	$137,500
Excess or (deficit)	$ -0-	($5,000)	($5,000)

BUDGET #2

Unrestricted funds have been shifted from home season to touring in order to create "need" in home season. Home season budget can now be submitted to funding source with statement of need.

Account	Home Season	Touring	Total
INCOME			
Ticket Sales	$57,500	$ 5,000	$ 62,500
Road Fees	-0-	45,000	45,000
National Endowment	-0-	5,000	5,000
State Arts Council	10,000	-0-	10,000
Individuals	5,000	5,000	10,000
TOTAL	$72,500	$60,000	$132,500
EXPENSES			
Salaries	$56,000	$21,500	$ 77,500
Living Allowance	-0-	18,000	18,000
Travel Expenses	-0-	8,000	8,000
Scenery, Etc.	8,000	2,000	10,000
Truck	500	4,500	5,000
Promotion	2,000	2,000	4,000
Administration	11,000	4,000	15,000
TOTAL	$77,500	$60,000	$137,500
Excess or (deficit)	($5,000)	$ -0-	($5,000)

Note: Project budgets can be summed to one total organizational (or single fund) budget. In this case, while the organizational budget remains constant, the project budgets are quite different in the two versions.

of the opera company that he is not interested in supporting the company's touring activities but would be willing to make a contribution toward programs in the local community. The opera company director, with the approval of the board, can now prepare a new budget with ticket sale revenue shifted out of the home season category into the touring category. This creates a shortfall in the home season, which is necessary in the official request to the foundation.

Using this same approach, the opera company can even project an overall surplus for the organization and still show a need for funds for a particular activity. The director, with the approval of the board, prepares a budget that includes a "Reserve Fund" category (see Figure 5.3). Income is shifted into the reserve fund thereby creating the appropriate deficits in other parts of the operation. When the director of the foundation says that his organization is prepared to make a $30,000 contribution to the home season, a budget is prepared that shows a shortfall of exactly that amount in that category. Meanwhile, the organization banks a healthy surplus for the year.

FIGURE 5.3. Project Budgeting
Compton Opera Company

In this example, the organization created a deficit position in the home season even after receiving the foundation grant by shifting unrestricted funds to its "reserve fund." Now it can attempt to raise even more money for its "deficit" by submitting the home season budget to the funding source.

	Home Season	Touring	Reserve Fund	Total
INCOME				
Ticket Sales	$32,500	$ 5,000	$25,000	$ 62,500
Road Fees	-0-	45,000	-0-	45,000
National Endowment	-0-	5,000	-0-	5,000
State Arts Council	10,000	-0-	-0-	10,000
Friendly Foundation	5,000	-0-	-0-	5,000
Individuals	-0-	5,000	5,000	10,000
TOTAL	$47,500	$60,000	$30,000	$137,500
EXPENSES				
Salaries	$56,000	$21,500	$ -0-	$ 77,500
Living Allowance	-0-	18,000	-0-	18,000
Travel Expenses	-0-	8,000	-0-	8,000
Scenery, etc.	8,000	2,000	-0-	10,000
Truck	500	4,500	-0-	5,000
Promotion	2,000	2,000	-0-	4,000
Administration	11,000	4,000	-0-	15,000
TOTAL	$77,500	$60,000	$ -0-	$137,500
Excess or (Deficit)	($30,000)	-0-	$30,000	-0-

Note: That as a single fund budget (last column), the organization has balanced income and expense. However, the fund raiser can still go out and raise $30,000 for the home season's "deficit."

People who work in nonprofit organizations are sometimes nervous about manipulating numbers in this way. They worry that the procedure may not be appropriate or even legal. Some think that nonprofits must lose money—or at best, break even—to meet the legal requirements. This is a fundamental misunderstanding of the nonprofit concept. A *surplus* (that is, an excess of income over expenditure) is not only legal, it is desirable. If it were not, how would it have been possible for the established universities, churches, art museums, and other nonprofits to build such large reserves in the form of endowments over the years? While these surpluses are legal, however, profits are not. A *profit* is another name for "owner's equity." The organization's owner (or partner or shareholder) benefits directly when the organization makes money. He may take the profit in cash or the distribution may be deferred; but in any case, a direct benefit inures to the person who has the financial interest. Nonprofit organizations do not have owners, of course, and they do not have shareholders. They serve the public, and so any excess of income over expenditure must ultimately be used for a charitable purpose. The word *ultimately* is important here. The money does not have to be spent right away. It can be put away in some kind of reserve fund or into an endowment (which is simply a reserve fund that has specific restrictions on when and/or how the assets are to be used). This "putting away" process is highly desirable and all organizations should strive to put some money away each year.

CONTINGENCY/RESERVE

Generating enough excess income in order to put money away can be facilitated by the budget process. A nonprofit organization should create an account called "contingency/reserve" that it lists on the expense side of its budget. The amount budgeted on this line should equal as much as 5 percent of the organization's total income (see Figure 5.1). Thus, if a nonprofit organization has a budget of $84,000 for the year, as is the case in Figure 5.1, it would reserve out $4,200 (or 5 percent) and allocate only $79,800 for its regular ongoing expenses. (For larger budget organizations, a smaller percentage can be allocated to contingency/reserve.)

What is the contingency/reserve line item used for? First, it can serve as a form of self-insurance in case some unexpected expense comes up during the year. This is the "contingency" portion. The Compton Opera Company finds that there is a bad storm on the night of the big "Aida" production and single ticket sales come in $2,000 under budget—the contingency/reserve line item takes care of it. Or, someone trips on the front stoop of the Compton School and sues which leads to an unexpected attorney's fee of $1,000. Once again, the organization has a pocket of uncommitted money from which it can draw.

If at the end of the fiscal year there is still money left after all contingencies have been taken care of, the line item becomes a "reserve." In other words, the unallocated money can be put away in some kind of savings instrument—a savings account, money market funds, stock—as determined by the board of directors on the advice of a financial professional. Each year, funds should be set aside in such a reserve until such time as the organization is one year ahead financially; that is, could operate an entire year without any income of any kind.

Why preach such fiscal conservatism? Anyone familiar with the statistics on the plight of nonprofit organizations knows that a great number go bankrupt within the first decade of existence. Ambitious programs get designed with inadequate financial reserves. Inflation and other factors lead to larger and larger cash shortfalls. Prudent planning demands that an organization put away reserves to carry them through tough times.

Another reason to put money in reserve is related to fund raising. Many funders do not wish to be alone in their support for a project or a capital purchase. Others do not like to be the first to contribute. Reserve funds speak to both of these problems in the following way. Suppose you want to buy a new piece of equipment for a town park. It will cost $10,000. You wish to secure ten $1,000 gifts from wealthy individuals in the community. You know how difficult it will be to get the first contribution. So, you convince the board of directors of your organization to guarantee $3,000 from the reserve fund. You are now ready to make your first call. You tell the donor that you are trying to raise $10,000 and that you already have $3,000 in hand. The psychological effect is much more positive than telling the donor that he or she would be making the first contribution. In the end, if you do actually raise the whole $10,000 in contributions, you simply do not draw on the reserve funds.

Consider, alternatively, that you wish to embark on an exciting new training program for disadvantaged youth and the United States Department of Labor has agreed to give you $25,000 on a matching basis. Because the project is a new one, you cannot find any corporation, foundation, or group of individuals to provide the matching funds. However, you and your board of directors are convinced that the project is important and will ultimately be entirely fundable by outside sources. You decide to draw the matching funds out of your reserve fund. After a year, the project is deemed successful. Now with favorable press material, a positive outside evaluation, and other critical acclaim, you can approach the same funding sources with greater success.

Finally, there is another reason why the reserve fund is so important. Most nonprofit organizations experience cash flow problems at some time during the fiscal year as is discussed at the end of this chapter. Put another way, these organizations find that they need to pay bills before there is adequate income to do so. Often salaries and heavy capital expenditures place heavy cash demands on the budget early in the year while funding sources are slow to come through with the cash. It is embarrassing to find the organization in a position where it cannot pay bills or meet its payroll especially when the board has been so responsible about designing a conservative budget. One alternative is to borrow money. This alternative is usually expensive unless the organization can draw on the largesse of a wealthy friend or board member who will make an interest-free loan. On the other hand, with an adequate reserve fund, the organization can borrow from itself. That is, it can take money from the reserve fund early in the year and replenish it later when the projected income is finally received. It is important to remember, though, that even this procedure has a real cost. By taking money out of a reserve fund, the organization is foregoing certain income by forfeiting interest. It is important to keep this in mind so that the staff does not become cavalier about drawing on the reserves. It is always better to maximize a good cash flow position by doing adequate cash flow planning several months before the beginning of the fiscal year.

THE BUDGETING PROCESS

If budgeting is a form of financial planning, then it is important to know what specific procedures are involved in doing it effectively. There are two important considerations.

1. Budgeting should always be related to the overall planning process of the organization. No one is in a position to plan for the future without a clear sense of what the available resources are. Conversely, sensible budgets, or financial plans, cannot be put together without knowing where the organization is going. Simply allocating money is not enough. Using it strategically is what the budgeting process ideally should be about.

2. The board of directors should be involved in every step of both the budgeting and general planning process. Because board members must set long-range goals for the organization, decide on program priorities, and ultimately assume fiscal accountability, it is important that they be involved in the budgeting process both in the forecasting stages and later when the budget must be monitored.

Beyond these general considerations, there are eight steps that an organization should take to complete a successful budgeting cycle. These steps are as follows.

STEP 1: MAKE A WISH LIST

The first step in budgeting has nothing to do with numbers or dollars. It concerns an annual review of what the organization wishes to accomplish in the year to come. At the beginning of the budget cycle, the board and staff should consider objectives for the upcoming year. What should we be doing? What would we like to do if cost was not an object? This step is essential because it forces the board of directors to think systematically about the organization's activities, its mission, and its programs. It provides an opportunity to review the purposes for which the organization was formed, its long-range goals and plans, and its short-term objectives. Making a wish list is fun because it does not require a close monitoring of costs. It is the last time in the budgeting process that such an opportunity presents itself.

STEP 2: COST OUT THE LIST

How much will it cost to carry out the activities listed in step 1? Obviously, there are some basic costs that have to be covered just to keep the organization going. There is the office, staff salaries, and costs of the basic programs that were done last year. Each of these must be carefully "costed." In addition, the costs of new activities will also have to be evaluated.

Costing is not an easy process. Traditionally, there have been two methods. The first, called the incremental budgeting method, leans heavily on information contained in previous years' budgets. If an organization is carrying out an activity that it has done for several years, then the easiest way to prepare a budget for the coming year is to add a percentage increment for inflation and other factors to the figures contained in the previous year's budget. The other costing method, called zero-based budgeting, requires that each line item of a budget be calculated anew; staff members are told that any item in the budget will be zero unless they can provide a full justification for some other figure.

Obviously, some combination of these two approaches is desirable in the budgeting process. The previous year's budget figures will be immensely helpful in estimating the coming year's. In addition, it is also important to look at financial statements from the current year to see how accurate the original budget projections were. However, each item in the budget should also be examined carefully without reference to another year's figures. An assessment should be made, item by item, of whether the expenditure is required and if so, how large it should be. In addition, new projects and activities require estimates for which the previous year's budget is not very helpful.

99

In costing out the "wish list" developed in step 1, two things are important to remember.

1. Costs should always be estimated on the high side. Add at least 10 percent to all expense figures. Those people who budget expenses at a level they think will be correct are almost always underbudgeted.

2. As you consider the costs of added programs and activities, remember that they will add to your central administrative costs. It is not enough simply to estimate how much you will actually spend on a new program. The simple addition of the program puts an added burden on the core staff, on space, on the typewriter, xerox machine, and so on.

As an example of how a new activity almost invisibly seems to increase central administrative costs, consider the case of the hospital that decided to undertake a prenatal education program. Staff members costed out all anticipated expenditures connected with the new program. However, they forgot that the hospital published an "Information Bulletin" in which each hospital class was given a one-page description. By adding the prenatal class, the hospital was required to add a page to a publication that was paid for out of the central administrative budget. It is crucial, as the costing process goes forward, that realistic overhead increases such as this are built into the budgets of new initiatives.

There are two ways an organization can deal with administrative costs. One is simply to create a major category called "Central Administration" and lump all salaries, rent, and other administrative expenses in this general category. Another approach is to engage in cost allocation (see Figure 5.4). Here the idea is to charge to each activity or program a reasonable percentage of central administrative costs. "How much of our museum director's time will be taken up by the new travelling exhibition program," an organization's board member might ask. If the answer is 10 percent of his time, then 10 percent of his salary is allocated to this program. Or the question might be, "what percentage of the photocopier and postage expenses should we allocate to the travelling exhibition program?" Again, the idea is to find a reasonable figure based on anticipated demand.

One advantage of cost allocation is that it assists the board and the staff in determining more accurately the actual costs of activities and programs. There is one cautionary note, however. Some people take cost allocation much too seriously. They count stamps, monitor phone calls, and keep logs of people's time. This may be useful for a day or a week to get a rough approximation on which a percentage can be developed for each program, but it can be overdone and result in much wasted time and frustration.

FIGURE 5.4. Compton Museum
Expense Projections with Administrative Costs Allocated to All Programs

	Education Program	Permanent Collection	Travelling Exhibition	Membership	Fund Raising	General Administration	TOTAL
Salaries	22,500	18,000	9,000	10,000	25,000	20,000	104,500
Benefits	3,375	2,700	1,350	1,500	3,750	3,000	15,675
Fees	16,000	2,000	0	0	5,000	4,000	27,000
Supplies	2,700	500	500	1,100	800	3,000	8,600
Telephone	300	600	600	500	200	2,000	4,200
Travel	0	50	700	100	2,000	2,000	4,850
Printing	2,000	2,000	2,000	2,000	2,000	2,000	12,000
Equipment	1,000	1,500	500	500	500	2,000	6,000
Shipping	0	500	2,000	0	0	0	2,500
Utilities	600	1,500	300	300	300	600	3,600
Insurance	800	11,000	5,000	200	200	1,000	18,200
TOTAL	49,275	40,350	21,950	16,200	39,750	39,600	207,125

In the budget projections above, administrative costs have not been lumped together in an administrative category but have been spread out over all categories based on an estimate of what each program or activity requires. This gives a clear sense of the *real* costs of the various activities.

STEP 3: ALLOCATE INCOME

Using the same list of activities developed in step 1 and costed out in step 2, it is now time to consider how much income can be expected from each activity. Again, last year's budget and the current year's financial statements can be helpful. This step is a bit tricky because there are certain funds specifically earmarked for a particular activity and other income that has no such restrictions and can be put anywhere.

Here it is important to understand the difference between *restricted* and *unrestricted* funds. Unrestricted funds are monies received with no particular instructions or limitations as to how they are to be used. Admission, memberships, earned income from publications or a shop, or general donations are all examples of unrestricted funds. Restricted funds, on the other hand, are those received with special limitations as to the time period or the purpose of their use. A grant for a new piece of equipment or a contribution to a scholarship fund can only be used for the purpose that the donor specified. Similarly, a grant for the fiscal year beginning July 1, 1984 cannot be used before that date nor after June 30, 1985. (One brief remark about restricted funds: An organization can always request that a donor lift or change a restriction. In fact, it is more common for restrictions to be changed than for funds to be returned to a donor.)

Once restricted funds and unrestricted funds have been separated, the process of allocating income is as follows (see Figure 5.5).

1. Put all restricted income into the proper program activity or category. That is, any income clearly attributable to a specific project should be put into that category and marked with an asterisk. Later on, when the board begins to cut out programs or activities, it is important to remember that these funds cannot be transferred from one program to another.

2. Cover all of the most basic administrative costs with unrestricted income.

3. Allocate the balance of unrestricted income across all the programs and activities listed. You may want to allocate it on a percentage basis in which case you calculate the fraction that each program expense total is of the total budget and use this fraction to calculate how much money should go to each program category. Or, you may want to use a simpler method and divide the money up on a roughly equal basis among programs. The first method, while more work, does help you assess the relative cost effectiveness of programs when you get to step 4 below. However, the second method is much less work. Ultimately, it does not matter how you allocate the unrestricted funds to programs and

FIGURE 5.5. Compton Museum
Income Projections with Restricted and Unrestricted Fund Separated

	Education Program	Permanent Collection	Travelling Exhibitions	Membership	Fund Raising	General Administration	TOTAL
Membership	—	5,350	—	16,200	7,500	7,500	36,550
Admissions	10,000	—	—	—	15,000	15,000	40,000
Rental Fees	—	—	14,000**	—	—	—	14,000
Tuition	28,500**	—	—	—	—	—	28,500
Museum Shop	—	—	—	—	7,500	7,500	15,000
Individual Donations	—	30,000*	—	—	9,750	9,600	49,350
Government Grants	—	5,000*	2,500*	—	—	—	7,500
Corporate Grants	2,500*	—	—	—	—	—	2,500
Foundation Grants	2,000*	—	—	—	—	—	2,000
Endowment Income	4,000*	—	1,000	—	—	—	5,000
TOTAL	47,000	40,350	17,500	16,200	39,750	39,600	200,400

*restricted gifts
**income generated by program
Note: Only unasterisked funds can be switched. If there is a decision to cut the Education Program, for example, only the $10,000 of unrestricted income from admissions can be switched. The balance is lost as income unless restrictions are lifted by donors. In any case, the museum would lose $28,500 in tuition fees.

103

projects *at this point* because you must make adjustments later on to put everything in balance.

4. Understate all income estimates by at least 10 percent. Just as you left some margin for error on expenses, so you must be equally conservative on income forecasting.

STEP 4: COMPARE

This is often called the "read it and weep" step. It should be clear by this time that some projects must be given up if the budget is going to balance. There is simply too much expense and not enough income. In fact, if the board discovers that income is adequate to cover expenditures *at this point* in the budgeting process, there should be great concern that the organization is not reaching far enough or being ambitious enough. Put another way, if the board can pay for all of its wishes, it is not wishing hard enough. Its reach should exceed its grasp so that it can continue to grow in its ability to provide services and programs to the public. However, the board is not acting responsibly when it *undertakes* more than it can pay for. Many projects should be considered even though only some will be undertaken immediately. The examination of a potential activity one year is valuable in planning for that activity another year.

In comparing one program activity to another, the board can use the criterion of cost effectiveness. Which activities come closest to paying for themselves? Which have the highest cost relative to the income they bring in? These are the kinds of questions that are asked in profit-making companies, and they are certainly of more than passing interest to any nonprofit organization. However, there is also a danger here. Remember that nonprofit organizations are not in business primarily to make money. Their missions may dictate that they carry on certain activities that are *not* cost effective. How would we feel, for example, if the only activities engaged in by a certain church were its profitable rummage sales and Bingo games. We (and, most likely, the Internal Revenue Service) would be concerned that a more fundamental mission of the church was not being fulfilled. Thus, cost effectiveness, while one criterion, is only one. The primary criterion should relate to the mission of the organization, its purposes, goals, and objectives.

STEP 5: SET PRIORITIES

Any board member or staff person who has sat through a budget session in which programs and projects are debated for inclusion in the next year's budget knows what a difficult session it can be. Some people, who may have been silent for a time, suddenly emerge with a pet project that simply must be included. Others, wishing to be more fiscally restrained, may urge the board to reject any new activities. In the end, a priority setting session *must* relate not solely to dollars and cents but to a fundamental assessment of the organization's reason for being. It is too easy in the heat of the moment to argue for or against an activity on its own merits or on cost effectiveness. But it is important to ask: "Is this activity really central to what we are about? Does it help us get where we want to be in a year? in two years? in five years? Is it more important to build up a reserve to protect the organization over the long term?" These are difficult questions, but in asking them the board is fulfilling a fundamental role in deciding what course is best for the organization and most clearly in the public interest.

STEP 6: ADJUST AND BALANCE

Once activities have been put in some semblance of priority order, a little negotiation is still possible as the budget is adjusted and put into balance. If the Compton Museum's Travelling Exhibition Program is a high priority but there is simply not quite enough to cover it, perhaps some money can come out of the "Acquisitions" budget. If the program is dropped instead, monies that were allocated to it can be moved to other areas if those monies are unrestricted. One must be careful, obviously, not to move monies that can only be used for the travelling exhibition program itself. For example, if there is a grant for that program or if there was income projected from exhibition rentals, that income is now lost to the organization.

Until now, our budget has been skewed conservatively. We have understated income, overstated expenses, and saved out 5 percent of our total income for the contingency/reserve category. Even though the budget is balanced on paper, it would appear that there is far more money coming in than going out. Careful budgeting, however, requires this approach. It is almost always the case that certain expenses have been forgotten, and certain anticipated income comes in short. In the event that the actual financial picture results in income far exceeding expenses, the board has the enviable task of deciding what to do with the additional money.

STEP 7: APPROVE

Now that the budget has been worked out, it is necessary for the full board of directors to discuss and approve it. This is more than a mere formality. In voting through a budget, the board exercises its fiduciary responsibility in setting financial limits and boundaries for the staff. The board is also implicitly agreeing to make sure that the projected revenues will be forthcoming, particularly those funds that have to be raised. A board of directors should never approve a budget "based on a wish and a prayer" that projects unrealistic fund-raising goals. If such a budget is approved, and the funds are not raised, it is the trustees who must take responsibility. Thus, a good question to ask during the "approval" process is: "Do we really know how every projected revenue dollar will be earned or raised, who will be responsible, and whether the targets are realistic?"

On the expense side, a responsible board member should ask how estimates were determined. For example, if the line item for postage is $2,500 and the board member is told by staff that the number was arrived at by taking last year's figure, a good question might be, "Is that a realistic figure given the fact that postal rates have increased by 20 percent and we have added 300 people to our mailing list?"

Indeed, because the previous year's budget is so often the primary document upon which so many estimates are made, it is easy for the budget preparers to forget to take obvious changes into consideration. Trustees should challenge the budget document, not because they doubt the ability of the staff, but because it is they, not the staff, who are ultimately responsible for the fiscal health of the organization.

STEP 8: MONITOR AND AMEND

One common mistake in the budget process is to assume it has come to an end once the board approves the final document. Indeed, the very word *final* is a misnomer when talking about a budget. Few budgets can hold up over time unless they are amended and modified to accommodate new information and new conditions as the year wears on. For this reason, board and staff must set up a process by which the budget can be reviewed when necessary and changed.

Two extremes should be avoided. The board should not insist that the document they have approved "is it" and force the staff to stick to it without modifiction throughout the fiscal year. On the other hand, the board should not be willing to say that the budget document is only a "rough approximation" and give staff instructions to "come as close as possible." Rather, a formal, documented procedure should be set up that allows staff some flexibility but gives the board the final say on any significant changes in the budget figures.

For example, in a $100,000 budget, the board may tell the executive director the following (which would be documented in the minutes of the board meeting at which it was approved): "So long as you feel you can balance the budget, you may shift up to 15 percent or $2,000 (whichever is less) out of or into any account. However, if more significant changes are to be made, you must present a revised budget to the board for approval."

By way of example, let us say that the line item "Equipment" has a budgeted amount of $20,000. Using the guidelines previously listed, the director may, at his or her discretion and without board approval, move up to $2,000 to some other expenditure category or may choose to spend $2,000 more in that category. The director should not do the extra spending however unless he or she is relatively confident that the budget can still be balanced by additional income or by shifting the $2,000 from some other category where it is not needed. If the director anticipates that an additional $4,000 is necessary for equipment, then the full board must be consulted and an amended budget must be submitted and approved.

CONTROLS

These monitoring and amending procedures suggest that the trustees should be consulted on any significant change in the budget. However, a "suggestion" alone is not sufficient. It does not assure the trustees that such consultation will take place. Nor does it assure a funder that the board is in a position to monitor carefully the staff's spending of its dollars. Finally, it does not address the question of how money will be handled internally to assure that it will be safely received, recorded, deposited, and expended in a manner that the trustees deem appropriate. In this area, the area of controls on budget monitoring and on the handling of money and financial transactions, the trustees must set clear policies and make sure they are carried out.

Fortunately, guidelines exist on what is considered appropriate. Any responsible accountant can advise an organization on what is "generally accepted" as appropriate procedure. For example, many fiscal procedures are based on the notion that two people are far less likely to make a mistake, either intentionally or unintentionally, than one. So one kind of financial control is to be sure that two people are involved in transactions involving the receipt of cash, the preparation of financial statements, the expenditure of funds, and other financial matters. Here are some examples.

Controls on Incoming Monies: The person who opens the mail should record all incoming checks and cash and keep a list. Checks and cash should then be forwarded to the fiscal officer who prepares the deposit slip and keeps a record. Periodically, someone other than these two people (the board treasurer or the executive director) should check to see that the two sets of records agree.

Controls on Budget Monitoring: Two people should be involved in the processing of all outgoing money. One person who is familiar with the budget, the organization's operation, and the appropriateness of specific expenditures, should be responsible for *approving* payments. This person is often the director of the organization. Another person should actually write the checks and monitor the expenditures for the trustees. If the director stays within the budget, or the limits beyond the budget set by the board, a check can be written. If the director has approved payments beyond this amount, the matter must be referred to the treasurer, or finance committee, or full board for approval or for an amended budget.

A simple method for documenting the processing of payments requires that the organization invest in a rubber stamp with the following designations:

```
Date Received: _____
Date Paid: _____
Account: _____
Check Number: _____
Approved: _____
```

Every invoice, before it is paid, gets stamped. When no invoice exists for a particular item, such as a salary payment, a dummy invoice is prepared by staff and stamped. The executive director, or the person responsible for approving invoices, fills out the first, third, and bottom lines. The first line indicates the date the invoice was received, the third indicates the account or "line item" that the expense gets charged to, and the final line allows the director to indicate his or her approval of the payment with a signature. The person responsible for writing the checks fills out the second and fourth lines after making sure that there is enough money left in the account to pay the bill. After the completion of the transaction, the invoice is placed in a file so that an auditor can review the "paper trail" backing up the particular payment. For organizations with a fairly heavy volume of transactions, it is recommended that there be a separate file for each account.

Controls on "First Person" Payments: It is generally not recommended that the person who writes checks have the power to issue a check to himself or herself without at least a countersignature on the check. While banks probably will not monitor this, the policy can be recorded in the minutes of a board meeting and a person can be held in violation of a fiscal policy if the rule is not followed. Checks made out to "cash" should also be forbidden. In addition, all incoming money, whether of cash or check, should be deposited promptly in the organization's bank account before it is used to pay a bill.

Bonding: Bonding is a form of insurance that protects an organization from financial losses stemming from either intentional or unintentional irregularities in the handling of money. Generally, those people who handle money and/or sign checks are listed in the bonding document. Like any form of insurance, a limit is placed on the amount an organization can collect in the case of a loss. The greater the limit, the greater the annual premium. As a general rule of thumb, an organization should not use total annual expenses as the bonding limit figure even though at first glance this would seem to be prudent. The total budgeted dollars are rarely available to spend at any one time, and so it is unlikely that any loss would be so great. The organization should determine the maximum amount of money it anticipates having in the bank at any one time, increase the figure by 20 percent, and use that number as the bonding limit.

Some funding sources require evidence of bonding before they will contribute dollars to a nonprofit organization. Whether or not they do, it should be a comfort both to funders and to the trustees to know that such insurance against loss is in place. The board should remember that if an organization cannot make good on a loss, and bonding has not been provided, it is the trustees' own pocketbooks that are next in line for collection attempts.

CASH FLOW

"We prepared a conservative budget and thought we were in good shape. Three months into the fiscal year we found ourselves out of money. Bills were coming in faster than we received cash. The state agencies that provided tuition money for certain kids were often three to six months behind in their payments and the federal government wouldn't allow us to keep any of their funds on hand (we could only request what we had spent). We had never heard the term *cash flow* before but we sure learned the hard way what a cash flow problem is."

These words came from the director of a day care center. Her experience is not unusual. Like so many people who devise a sensible budget, she thought she would have no financial problems. She never thought about the fact that an annual budget only tells you how things should end up at the end of the year. It does not tell you how much cash you will have on hand at various points during the year. It is important to figure this out so you know whether you need to make some special arrangements in order to pay the bills.

Cash flow projections are most commonly prepared on a monthly basis for the upcoming fiscal year. In the analysis, an organization's income and expense are projected for each month. If you are not sure when a particular expenditure is going to be due, it is best to be conservative, plan for the worst, and figure that it is going to be due on the early side; to practice the same prudence with income, you should err on the late side in predicting when cash is going to come in. The budget is laid out on a wide sheet of paper and listed next to each line item is each of the monthly estimates. For example, if salaries for the year are $120,000, and if they do not change from month to month, the line item "Salaries" would appear with both its annual total of $120,000 and the various monthly totals of $10,000 next to it. The first three months would appear thus:

	Total	Jan	Feb.	March	etc.
Salaries . . .	$120,000	10,000	10,000	10,000	etc.

On the other hand, if all of the printing expenses come during the first month, the entry for printing would appear thus:

	Total	Jan.	Feb.	March	etc.
Printing . . .	$5,000	5,000	0	0	etc.

Once you have listed your estimated monthly income and expenses, you can compute your *monthly cash balances*. A monthly cash balance is simply the difference between income and expense during that month. If after preparing your monthly budget chart, you anticipate that your organization will take in $6,812 in July and spend $6,467, you will have a positive cash balance for July of $345. If for August you show income of $5,673 and expenses of $6,529, you will have a negative monthly cash balance of $856.

All of this is useful to know, but you still have not really analyzed your changes in cash flow position. What you really want to see is how the ups and downs of your monthly cash balances affect a cumulative flow of cash. The way this is done is shown in Figure 5.6. Under your monthly cash balance, you show how much cash you plan to have on hand at the beginning of the month. To this amount, called the *opening*

FIGURE 5.6. Hippy Dippy Day Care Cash Flow

	July	August
EXPECTED INCOME		
Parent Fees	2500	1810
Title XX	2211	2106
School Lunch Program	926	882
United Way	875	875
Fundraising	300*	0
Other Income	0	0
TOTAL INCOME	6812	5673
EXPECTED EXPENDITURES		
Staff Salaries	3468	3468
Substitutes	280	350
Fringe	544	556
Legal and Audit Fees	100	100
Program Development/Training	50	0
Rent/Mortgage	425	425
Utilities	50	40
Food	950	890
Equipment, Supplies, Services	200	550**
Insurance	250	0
Loan Repayment	150	150
TOTAL EXPENDITURES	6467	6529
MONTHLY CASH BALANCE	345	(856)
OPENING CASH BALANCE	200	545
CUMULATIVE CASH BALANCE	545	(311)

*4th of July fundraising profits
**includes $350 purchase of outdoor equipment
This example is taken from "Money Management Tools—Cash Flow Analysis"
by Roger Neugebauer in *Child Care Information Exchange,* Volume 19, May,
1981, p. 10.

cash balance, you add the monthly cash balance you calculated earlier
(the difference between income and expense for that month). The sum of
these two numbers is your *cumulative cash balance* or ending cash
balance for the month. This bottom line tells you where you stand at the
month's end and tells you how much you will have to start the next
month with. Thus, the cumulative cash balance for July becomes the
opening cash balance for August and so on.

If you do cash flow projections early enough (four to six months
before the start of the fiscal year), you are usually in a much better
position to solve a potential cash shortage problem. For example, you
might make a special plea to a funder to put you first on the payment list;
you might decide to do your fund-raising event earlier in the year; you
might negotiate with your printer to spread your payments over two

months rather than just one. People are generally much more flexible about these requests if you give them plenty of warning. By way of contrast, when the day of reckoning comes and you do not have cash to pay the bills, people become very impatient.

If all else fails and you will have a cash shortfall during the year, you have several alternatives. One is to take money from your reserve fund if you have one. For this reason, many organizations leave a substantial portion of their reserve in some liquid savings instrument so they can get at the cash quickly when they need it. If you do not have a reserve fund, you may be forced to borrow money for a short period of time. Ideally, a trustee (or several) might loan you the cash interest free. Otherwise, you will have to borrow from a bank, which can be extremely expensive. If cash must be borrowed and interest must be paid on the loan, be sure to build the interest payment into the expenses of your budget.

SUMMARY

We have reviewed the steps that must be taken to prepare for the fiscal year of a nonprofit organization. Once the actual period of the fiscal year was determined, we concentrated our attention on budget preparation. This activity involved both board and staff in general speculation about the future of the organization, as well as the detail work of preparing numbers for review. We then considered the kinds of monitoring procedures and financial controls that must be established before the organization is in a position to begin handling money responsibly. Finally, we examined how to develop cash flow projections so that embarrassing cash shortages can be avoided.

It cannot be stressed enough how important it is to engage in forward financial planning at all times. Planning for the fiscal year is an ongoing process of activities, not a one-time budget review session. Indeed, financial planning and monitoring for one year overlaps with the same activity for subsequent and/or previous years. As the cycle for one year progresses, the cycle for the next year begins. Like organizational planning, financial planning is a process with no real beginning or end.

6

Keeping Financial Records

Some people are rather casual about the way they maintain their personal financial records. They may write a check and forget to record it in the checkbook. They may reconcile their checking account at the end of the month and find that their records and the bank's disagree by a couple of dollars. Worse yet, upon discovering this, they may simply decide that "the bank is probably right" and enter the bank's figure in the checkbook. Or upon receiving a credit card statement, they may decide not to look for the charge receipts for each item and assume: "The statement is probably right . . . I'll just send in a check."

If individuals choose to conduct their financial affairs in such a lax way, no one is going to complain too much about it. But nonprofit organizations do not enjoy the same luxury. Records *must* be maintained carefully and should be reviewed periodically by an independent outside examiner who can certify that the organization is operating legally and according to generally accepted standards and procedures. Because the nonprofit organization is a kind of "public trust" (as we saw in Chapter 1) that enjoys numerous financially lucrative privileges and benefits, the organization must be able to demonstrate that its fiscal house is in order. It can only do so if its record keeping is accurate and its financial statements beyond reproach.

This chapter is an introduction to the subject of financial record keeping. It discusses how to choose accounting systems, how to keep books, and how to produce financial statements. The subject has its own special language, which is often difficult to the layperson, but the concepts themselves are logical once the terminology is mastered. It is important that every trustee and every nonprofit executive director try to master the basic concepts so that they can make informed financial decisions. They must be familiar with the *"generally accepted accounting procedures"* that financial people agree on as standards of proper financial record keeping. For it is on the basis of these standards that a certified public accountant determines whether the organization should be given a clean bill of health when an audit is conducted. It is also upon these standards that funders, prospective trustees, regulatory agencies, and others determine whether the organization is operating properly, deserves its tax-exempt status, and should receive financial support and other assistance.

ACCOUNTING

Accounting is the term used for financial record keeping. Another word for accounting is *bookkeeping*. There are two common accounting methods. The first, *cash basis accounting*, has the advantage of being simple and straightforward; the second, *accrual based accounting* is more complex but gives a more complete view of the organization's fiscal health.

Cash basis accounting: Most people are familiar with cash basis accounting because they do it when they maintain financial records for their checking and savings accounts. Financial transactions are recorded only when cash changes hands. When a person receives money and deposits it in the bank, the deposit is recorded as income and added to the bank account balance. When cash is withdrawn from the bank (or when a check is written which is the equivalent of a withdrawal), the transaction is recorded as an expense and the amount is subtracted from the bank account balance. The cash basis accounting system is quite straightforward if all a person needs to know is how much money is in the account. However, what it does not reveal is the financial health of the person maintaining the account, because it tells nothing about what that individual *owes* and how much *is owed* to him or her.

Accrual based accounting: For many individuals, credit cards have forced a kind of informal accrual based accounting into their personal systems of financial record keeping. This system takes into account what they owe and what is owed to them. Though few of us do formal accrual based accounting, a lot of us do something very much like it as we estimate whether or not we will have enough cash to pay the mortgage or rent during the next month. If we see a nice article of clothing and try to figure out whether we can afford it by thinking about our outstanding bills and yet-to-be-received paychecks, we are engaged in informal accrual based accounting.

Accrual based accounting recognizes expenses not only when money changes hands but also when *expenses* are incurred and income is *committed.* If the Compton Community Center purchases office supplies for $125 and tells the store to send a bill, an accrual based system recognizes the $125 as a financial obligation from the moment the purchase is made, and the amount is deducted from the organization's net worth. Similarly, if the Compton Community Center receives a letter from a funding agency that is an official notification of a $5,000 grant, the $5,000 is added to the net worth figure for the organization as soon as the letter is received. In the case of the $125 bill, the amount is called a *payable* until actually paid; thereafter, it becomes a regular expense. In the case of the $5,000 grant, the amount is called a *receivable* until the check is received and deposited; thereafter, it becomes normal revenue.

In the case just cited, if the Compton Community Center has

$3,000 in the bank on the day that it charges $125 worth of office supplies and receives the grant letter for $5,000, a cash basis accounting system indicates the organization's bank balance of $3,000. An accrual based accounting system, on the other hand, adds the $5,000 grant receivable and subtracts the $125 payable showing a net figure of $7,875, which is a truer picture of the organization's net worth.

It should be obvious that knowing the financial condition of an organization is more revealing than knowing its bank balance, if the organization's financial health is the main consideration. For example, an organization with no money in the bank borrows $30,000, pays $20,000 of outstanding bills, and deposits the remaining $10,000 in its bank account. On a cash basis, a financial accounting would only reveal a positive cash balance of $10,000. On an accrual basis, the outstanding loan of $30,000 would be taken into account and the organization would show a net worth of − $20,000. From the point of view of a prospective trustee, a funder, or anyone else attempting to assess the organization's fiscal health, the second figure would give a more accurate picture.

Choosing methods: Cash basis accounting is much simpler than the accrual method and provides most people in the organization with enough financial information. It keeps accurate track of income and outflow, and it tells people whether there is sufficient cash in the bank to pay the bills; yet, occasionally, the information from an accrual based system is also necessary. For that reason, many organizations, even those with budgets in excess of a million dollars, use what is called a *modified cash based accounting system.* According to this system, the books are kept on a cash basis except for a few accounts that are kept on accrual. Generally, these accounts include those in which regular and/or important outstanding obligations need to be monitored. For example, these accounts usually include *federal taxes payable* and the *state taxes payable* accounts, and the accounts that show how much money has been withheld from employees' salaries and needs to be paid to federal and state taxing authorities. Accounts kept on the accrual basis may also include what are called *plant fund accounts,* particularly when an organization is purchasing equipment, land, or buildings over a period of years. In such cases, it is advantageous to show the amount of the annual budget committed to (or "due") the plant fund for these long-term purchases. When accounts are maintained in this way, the obligated monies are factored into the accounting system so that the organization does not spend the cash on other things just because it happens to be sitting in the bank.

In a modified cash basis system, it is necessary, at least once a year, to convert all of the accounts to accrual. At the end of the fiscal year, as part of the annual audit, an accountant will take all the payables and receivables and factor them into the financial statements, thus allowing the organization to show its entire financial operation on an accrual system. It should be pointed out that this practice, that of presenting closing financial statements on an accrual basis, is one of the "generally accepted accounting procedures" approved by the accounting profession. Only very small organizations with budgets of $75,000 or less, should try to get by with closing statements that are not presented in this way. For organizations whose boards of trustees (or funders, or regulatory agencies) may require more frequent accrual based statements, the books can be converted to accrual more often, but it is rarely necessary.

FINANCIAL STATEMENTS

Just as accounting systems are standardized, so are financial statements. When trustees and others want to assess the organization's financial health, they will look at two financial statements, the *balance sheet* and the *income statement*. The health metaphor is appropriate here because the two statements are used as a diagnostic tool in much the same way medical reports are used. Consider, for example, a doctor wishing to diagnose a sick patient. The first thing a doctor checks is the patient's vital signs chart, which reports such things as temperature, pulse, and blood pressure as of a particular moment in time. The second thing the doctor checks is the patient's medical history, a document of the patient's health over the course of time. Neither record by itself is adequate. Two patients with the exact same vital signs may be in very different states of health—the one recovering from a serious illness, the other on the decline from previously good health. Unless the doctor can assess progress over time, a vital signs chart is inadequate. Yet, the medical history is not adequate by itself either. It may be fine to know how a patient has been treated for various ailments over a period of five to ten years, but without an up-to-date reading of the patient's vital signs, there is no way to assess the current state of health.

The balance sheet and the income statement serve the same function in the fiscal area as the vital signs chart and the medical history do in the health area. The balance sheet, like the vital signs chart, is similar to a freeze frame, a snapshot of the organization's financial condition as of a particular date (often the last day of the fiscal year). It summarizes what the organization owns, what it owes, what is owed to it, and how much is left over. The *income statement* is like the medical history. It summarizes financial activity over a period of time (often a year). Unlike the balance sheet, which tells only where the organization's finances stand as of a particular moment in time, the income statement helps the financial diagnostician determine whether the manner in which the organization arrived at that state was "healthy." Armed with the income statement, more formally referred to as the "Statement of Revenue, Expenditures, and Changes in Fund Balance," it is possible to determine whether the organization had a surplus, a deficit, made any unusually large expenditures, or had any revenue "windfalls."

Before looking at the balance sheet and income statement in more detail, one more term must be introduced, *fund balance*. A fund balance is an entry that appears both on the balance sheet and the income statement. It ties the two statements together. In both statements, it is found on the *bottom line* (though on a balance sheet an additional "balance entry" may sometimes be placed below it to show that the statement is in balance). In a profit-making corporation, the fund balance is referred to as profit, owner's equity, or "bottom line." In a nonprofit organization, where there are no owners and no profits, the fund balance shows the organization's financial net worth when all of its financial obligations are subtracted from all of its cash and noncash assets.

THE BALANCE SHEET

The *balance sheet* (see Figure 6.1) is so called because each half adds up to the same total number. One half of the balance sheet (shown at the top of the statement) lists all of the organization's *assets* (that is, everything that the organization owns). The other half (shown on the bottom of the statement) lists both the organization's *liabilities* (everything that it owes) as well as its *fund balance*. Thus the "balance" in a balance sheet is between assets on the one hand and liabilities and fund balance on the other. Put in mathematical form:

Assets equal Liabilities plus Fund Balance: (A = L + FB)

Understanding this formula, we can easily see how the fund balance itself is calculated. If we know how much we own and how much we owe, then the fund balance is simply the difference between the two numbers or rearranging the previous mathematical formula:

Fund Balance equals Assets minus Liabilities: (FB = A − L)

Let us look more closely at a balance sheet to find out what it is really telling us. First, look at the "Assets" section of the statement in Figure 6.1. Assets are what the organization owns: cash in the bank, land,

FIGURE 6.1. Balance Sheet

ASSETS	
Cash	$ 1,101
Accounts Receivable	211
Prepaid Expenses	1,016
Land and Buildings	50,000
Total Assets	$52,328
LIABILITIES AND FUND BALANCE	
Liabilities	
Accounts Payable	$ 532
Notes Payable	11,012
Mortgage	25,221
Total Liabilities	$36,765
Fund Balance	$15,563
Total Liabilities and Fund Balance	$52,328

buildings, a collection of paintings, equipment (like typewriters and copier machines). In addition, because balance sheets are commonly prepared on an accrual basis, all the money owed to the organization is counted as an asset. These are called the "receivables" and might include things like grants on which the letter of commitment but not the check has been received or items sold and invoiced but for which the organization has not received payment.

Prepaid expenses are another category counted as assets. An example of a prepaid expense is a rental security deposit. Technically, the amount paid to the landlord is a prepayment for the final month or two of rent or for damage that may occur to the space. Because neither of these events has occurred at the time the balance sheet is prepared, the actual obligation to the landlord has not been incurred at that time. For this reason, the payment should technically not be subtracted from the organization's net worth. In order to compensate for this, and to give a more realistic picture of the organization's financial health, the prepaid expenses are added back to the "assets" total.

Moving to the other half of the balance sheet, there is a listing of all of the organization's liabilities (what it owes). On the first line under "Liabilities" are all of the unpaid bills (the accounts payable). Next are the longer term obligations such as outstanding loans (the notes payable). Finally, the principal balance of the mortgage is shown.[1] All of

[1]The balance sheet allows someone to calculate the equity of property owned by the organization. The value of the property is shown under "Assets" and the outstanding debt on the property is shown under "Liabilities." The amount of equity in the property is the difference between these two figures. Thus, in Figure 6.1, the equity is calculated as $50,000 minus $25,221, or $24,779. Interest payments do not appear on the balance sheet but are shown on the income statement.

these liability categories are then totalled and the sum is subtracted from total assets. The resulting difference produces the fund balance.

What does all of this information tell us? Beginning with the fund balance, we know the organization's net worth. In the case of the organization whose balance sheet is shown in Figure 6.1, the net worth is $15,563. Often a large fund balance connotes a healthy organization. But not always, and this is precisely the reason why the other numbers on the balance sheet are so important. In Figure 6.1 for example, the organization shows a fairly sizable fund balance. But upon closer examination we see that the reason for this is because it owns land and buildings. Its cash position is poor. It has only $1,101 in the bank and owes $11,544 (exclusive of the mortgage). In one sense, the organization could be called healthy. If it sold its land and buildings it could pay its debts and have plenty of money left over. On the other hand, if it hangs on to the property, it will have to raise a good deal of cash to pay its debts. Generally speaking, an organization that has to sell assets to pay debts is not considered financially healthy.

The balance sheet is an excellent tool for prospective trustees, funders, regulators, and others to decide whether the organization is a good financial risk. For the prospective trustee, the idea of joining a debt-ridden organization is usually not attractive; for potential funders, organizations with large accumulated deficits may be so preoccupied with their debts that they cannot focus on their programs and other activities; for the regulator, the monitoring of restricted fund use in financially troubled organizations becomes even more crucial as the temptation grows to find money to cover shortfalls.

The balance sheet can be most important to trustees and employees of an organization as a diagnostic tool if there is an understanding of how to use it. Unfortunately, many people are mystified by the statement and ignore it. They are content to study the income statement, which is more familiar to them and easier to understand. Because the income statement has a fund balance (or net worth) figure as well, the assumption is that it contains all the information they really need to know. But this is not the case, as we have just seen. An organization may have a very large fund balance and be heavily in debt. Only the balance sheet will reveal this. Consider the following case.

> Before joining the board, a prospective art museum trustee asked what the net worth of the institution was and was told that the figure was $2 million. Content that he was joining a financially healthy organization, he agreed to serve on the board. Later, when he was shown the balance sheet he was shocked. The museum owed over $1 million. However, its collection was valued at over $3 million, hence the high net worth figure. Because the museum could not deacquisition (that is, sell) any of

the works in the collection, the collection's value had little meaning as equity against debt. The trustee spent the next three years as a full-time fund raiser, something he had hoped he would not have to do when he joined the board.

Had this trustee studied the balance sheet before joining the board, he would have had a more complete picture of the organization's financial situation.

THE INCOME STATEMENT

If the balance sheet tells us what we need to know about an organization's financial health as of a particular moment in time, why is another financial statement necessary? The reason is simply that we not only need to know what the organization's health is today but must view the progress of that health over time. Two organizations may have identical balance sheets but one may be improving its financial condition and the other's financial health may be rapidly deteriorating. The income state-

FIGURE 6.2 Statement of Revenues, Expenditures, and Changes in Fund Balance

Revenues	
Membership	$14,225
Tuition	26,234
Government Grants	12,000
Corporate Gifts	15,750
Individual Donations	12,655
Other	11,222
Total Income	$92,086
Expenditures	
Salaries and Benefits	32,213
Professional Fees/Contractual	21,123
Office Supplies/Telephone	2,987
Travel and Subsistence	5,531
Printing and Promotion	7,298
Educational Materials	4,091
Utilities and Insurance	2,755
Mortgage Interest	6,643
Grounds Maintenance	4,000
Other	3,834
Total Expenditures	$90,475
Excess of Revenues Over Expenditures	$ 1,611
STARTING FUND BALANCE	$13,952
ENDING FUND BALANCE	$15,563

ment shows these financial trends *over time* and gives the historical perspective, which the balance sheet ignores.

Historical perspective is not the only value of an income statement. It also gives an idea of an organization's income sources and its expenditures. Revenues and expenditures are subdivided into categories that reveal such things as how much of the organization's income is earned, how dependent the organization is on government funding, how much is spent on personnel, or how much it costs to maintain the physical plant.

Unlike a balance sheet, in which the various entries are predictable and similar, the various revenue and expenditure categories on the income statement vary from one organization to another. (The categories usually closely parallel an organization's budgetary chart of accounts.) However, the final three lines shown in Figure 6.2 should appear on *every* income statement. The first of these entries, "Excess (or Deficit) of Revenues over Expenditures," shows whether the organization had a surplus or deficit for the year; it is calculated by subtracting total expenditures from total revenues. The next line, "Starting Fund Balance," gives the fund balance figure for the start of the fiscal period covered. (For example, if an income statement covers the year beginning January 1, 1983, the starting fund balance is the same as the ending fund balance for the year ending December 31, 1982 and can be found on last year's balance sheet or income statement.) The bottom line, "Ending Fund Balance," is simply the sum of the previous two entries and gives the final fund balance figure for the year. As we have already seen, this is the same number that appears on the balance sheet.

The income statement, like the balance sheet, is an important tool in analyzing the financial health of an organization. Knowing how to read the two statements and knowing what the various categories mean is extremely useful. It is also valuable to know the origin of the various numbers. For that reason, the rest of this chapter is devoted to a discussion of the manner in which financial transactions are recorded and financial statements are prepared.

THE BOOKS

Most people have heard the expression "keeping the books." Historically, it referred to the maintenance of financial records in actual books called *journals*. Each type of journal was a separate book, and each page was maintained for a particular purpose. Today, with the advent of computerized record keeping, records are not always kept in books. In any event, the terminology remains, and the bookkeeper must be familiar with the use of four types of books: the cash receipts journal, the cash disbursements journal, the general journal, and the general ledger.

The first three books actually have the word *journal* in their names. A *journal* is a book of *original entry* in which financial transactions are *initially recorded* and from which they are transferred (the technical term is *posted*) to another book called the *general ledger*. If the three journals are kept accurately, the financial affairs of the organization will be in order. This is because all subsequent financial records draw their information from these three books. Thus, an organization should make sure that the procedures are in place to keep the journals accurately and in a timely manner.

The *cash receipts journal* is the book in which all transactions involving incoming money are recorded. When cash or checks are received by the organization, they are recorded in the cash receipts journal.

The *cash disbursements journal* is the book in which all the organization's payments are recorded. When a check is written, it is recorded in the cash disbursements journal.

The *general journal* is the book in which all noncash transactions are recorded. Corrected errors, transfers between accounts, and accruals are recorded in the general journal.

In addition to the three journals, there is another book called the *general ledger* (the book of final entry). Although this book is a useful tool in financial management, it contains no new financial information and thus can be produced at any time by someone either inside the organization or from the outside. However, this is only possible if the person has access to correct information from the three journals. The general ledger cannot be produced unless the journals are maintained carefully and painstakingly.

In the *general ledger,* the information collected in the three journals is reorganized into a different form. It is summarized account by account. In organizations where the general ledger is still an actual physical book, one page is generally reserved for each account. On each page, the organization records the activity, month by month, of a particular line item—"salaries," for example—by taking the total activity for that account from the cash receipts journal, the cash disbursements journal, and the general journal. Once this information is summarized in the ledger, various further rearrangements of it can be made in order to compute the fund balance and produce the income statement and the balance sheet.

DOUBLE-ENTRY BOOKKEEPING

When we record deposits and checks in our checkbook records, we use what is called a *single entry* bookkeeping system. It is a system that helps us keep track of how much cash we have. Unfortunately, the system does not tell us how much we have spent or received in each category of expenditure or revenue. For example, there is no way in our checkbook records to summarize how much of our total income came from salary, from interest, from gifts, from rents, from bequests, or from other sources. Similarly, we have no way of knowing the total amount we have spent on food, on rent or on clothing. However, there is a system of bookkeeping that helps us keep track both of our cash on the one hand and our categories of income and expenditure on the other. It is called a *double-entry* system and it has the added advantage of being able to record transfers between accounts as well as computing, with very little effort, the basic information for the income statement and the balance sheet.

Unfortunately, the double-entry system is fraught with old terminology that confuses people. Unlike the word *journal,* which has a linguistic connection with the word *book,* the terms *debit* and *credit* in the double-entry bookkeeping system do not always mean what one might think they should mean. We generally think of a credit as something that increases value and a debit as something that decreases value. But in bookkeeping, the terms *credit* and *debit* do not refer to increasing or decreasing value in any simple and straightforward sense.

Credits and debits are simply two opposing entries in a two-way, self-balancing bookkeeping system. The system records financial transactions in such a way that two accounts are affected at once. The double-entry system should be thought of as a kind of balance scale in which equal weights must be added or subtracted from both sides in order to keep the scale in balance. In the bookkeeping system, the units used to keep the system in balance are credits and debits. The trick is in realizing that the terms *credit* and *debit* do *not* mean respectively units that are added and units that are subtracted. Rather both credits and debits will be added in certain circumstances and subtracted in others. One rule of thumb can be gleaned by the following chart:

CHART 6.A

	debit	credit
In the cash receipts journal	: cash	noncash account
In the cash disbursements journal	: noncash account	cash

The concept is easier to understand with specific examples. Consider an organization that has just received a check from the National

Endowment for the Arts, a government funding agency, in the amount of $5,000. In a double-entry system, we must enter the number $5,000 twice, once as a credit and once as a debit. Because the transaction involves the receipt of money, the place to record it is in the cash receipts journal. Referring to Chart 6.A, we find that the number should first be entered in the column marked "cash" as a *debit* and then in a "noncash account" column as a *credit*. (To figure out what account should be credited, we can check the organization's chart of accounts, given in Chart 6.B, and we find an appropriate account marked "Government Grants"). The transaction is entered in the cash receipts journal in the manner shown in Figure 6.3.

This organization must also pay its part-time secretary, Carolyn

CHART 6.B Chart of Accounts

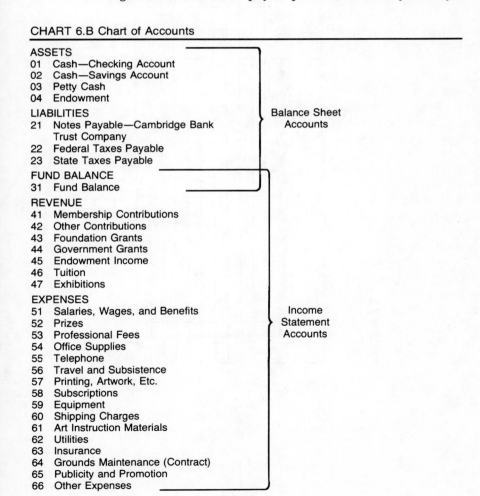

ASSETS
01   Cash—Checking Account
02   Cash—Savings Account
03   Petty Cash
04   Endowment

LIABILITIES   Balance Sheet
21   Notes Payable—Cambridge Bank   Accounts
      Trust Company
22   Federal Taxes Payable
23   State Taxes Payable

FUND BALANCE
31   Fund Balance

REVENUE
41   Membership Contributions
42   Other Contributions
43   Foundation Grants
44   Government Grants
45   Endowment Income
46   Tuition
47   Exhibitions

EXPENSES
51   Salaries, Wages, and Benefits   Income
52   Prizes   Statement
53   Professional Fees   Accounts
54   Office Supplies
55   Telephone
56   Travel and Subsistence
57   Printing, Artwork, Etc.
58   Subscriptions
59   Equipment
60   Shipping Charges
61   Art Instruction Materials
62   Utilities
63   Insurance
64   Grounds Maintenance (Contract)
65   Publicity and Promotion
66   Other Expenses

FIGURE 6.3.

CASH RECEIPTS JOURNAL

DATE	ACCOUNT CREDITED	EXPLANATION	CASH DEBIT	ACNT. 41 CREDIT	ACNT. 42 CREDIT	ACNT. 44 CREDIT	ACNT. 46 CREDIT
2/12	Government Grants	National Endowment grant #222	5000 -			5000 -	

126

FIGURE 6.4.

CASH DISBURSEMENTS JOURNAL

PAGE 1

DATE	CH.* NO.	PAYEE	ACCOUNT DEBITED	ACNT. 51 DEBIT	ACNT. 61 DEBIT	ACNT. 65 DEBIT	CASH CREDIT
2 1/2	213	Carolyn Stewart	Salaries	612 —			612 —

*Indicates check number.

127

Stewart, her salary for the month. A check is issued in the amount of $612. Referring to Chart 6.A, we see that the amount is first entered as a *debit* to a noncash account (in this case, referring to Chart 6.B, we see that the appropriate account is the one marked "Salaries, Wages, and Benefits"); second, it will be entered as a *credit* to "cash." To see how this transaction is accomplished in the cash disbursements journal, refer to Figure 6.4.

When do credits actually increase the value of a column and when do they decrease it? Conversely, how do debits affect the value of a column? The answer is that it depends on what kind of account category is being affected. Keep in mind that there are only five different kinds of accounts. There are three kinds found on the balance sheet—asset accounts, liability accounts, and fund balance—and the three kinds on the income statement—revenue accounts, expenditure accounts, and fund balance. (Because the fund balance appears on both statements, there are only five separate categories.) Chart 6.B organizes the chart of accounts into balance sheet accounts and income statement accounts. Chart 6.C shows how credits and debits change the value of the various kinds of accounts.

CHART 6.C

	debits	credits
Assets	increase	decrease
Liabilities	decrease	increase
Fund Balance	decrease	increase
Revenues	decrease	increase
Expenditures	increase	decrease

Let us go back to our examples to verify them against Chart 6.C. Our grant from the National Endowment for the Arts, which increased our revenues and our assets, was entered as a debit to "cash." Because "cash" is an *asset* account, and because a *debit increases our assets*, the net effect was the expected increase. The corresponding *credit* to our "grants" account, which is a *revenue account*, had the net effect of *increasing our revenues*, which is also what we would expect.

In the second transaction, the secretary was paid $612. By entering the $612 as a *credit* to cash (which is an *asset account*), we *decreased our assets*. Correspondingly, we entered the $612 as a *debit* to the "salary" account (which is an *expenditure account*), and thus *increased expenses*, as we should expect.

RECORDING TRANSACTIONS

As complex as all this may sound, the actual recording of the transactions is simple. The appropriately lined and labelled pages for cash receipts and cash disbursements journals (similar to those shown in Figures 6.3 and 6.4) are available from most stationery stores. Once an organization's chart of accounts has been set up, the entries into the books are a fairly routine matter.

Why, one might ask, is it worth doing all this? What is the point of making two entries for every financial transaction? One reason is that it is easier to produce the income statement and the balance sheet from a double-entry system. But there is another reason as well that can be gleaned by looking at the third journal, the *general journal*. It is here, in a double-entry bookkeeping system, that we can correct errors, make transfers between accounts, record accruals, and enter any transaction that does not involve cash. Such versatility is simply not possible in a single-entry bookkeeping system.

For example, suppose we had misread the amount of the National Endowment for the Arts' grant check and that instead of being $5,000 it had been $5,500. Before we discovered the error, we had already sent the check and deposit slip to the bank and recorded the amount as $5,000 in the cash receipts journal. When the bank statement came back, we found that the actual amount deposited was $5,500. At that point, it was too late to change the original entry (one should not go back and erase entries once they have been recorded). Thus, the only way to correct the mistake was to find a way to increase both our "cash" (asset) account and our "government grants" (revenue) account. Looking at Chart 6.C, it is clear that to accomplish this we will have to debit "cash" and credit "government grants" so that both will be increased. This is done in the *general journal* as is shown in Figure 6.5.

Now imagine that the $612 "salary" check to the secretary was not really a salary at all but was a "professional fee" because we did not withhold taxes and the secretary is really only a temporary replacement working as an independent contractor. In order to correct the miscategorization of the original payment, we have to transfer the transaction from one expense account to another in the *general journal*. We need to replace the $612 in the salary account (which means crediting that account to increase it) and we will charge the payment to the "professional fees" account (which means debiting that account). All of this is shown in Figure 6.5.

Finally, suppose we need to show an accrual, such as a tax obligation to the government. Once again, we would do this in the

FIGURE 6.5.

GENERAL JOURNAL   PAGE 1

DATE		ACCOUNT TITLES AND EXPLANATION	FO-LIO	DEBIT	CREDIT
2	28	01- Cash		500 —	
		44 - Government Grants			500 —
		(to correct deposit error)			
2	28	51- Salaries			612 —
		53- Professional Fees		612 —	
		(to reassign check #.213 from			
		"salary" to "fee")			
2	28	22 - Federal Taxes Payable			331 —
		51- Salaries		331 —	
		(to record accrued tax			
		obligation on salary payments)			

130

general journal. Imagine that the organization owes $331 in federal taxes. Because the money is not yet due, we have not written the check, nor recorded an actual payment in the cash disbursements journal. However, it is important that the obligated money not be spent on something else; thus, we will show the $331 as a "payable." To do so, we must increase one of our liability accounts, the "Federal Taxes Payable" by $331. Looking at Chart 6.C, we see that the only way to increase a liability account is to credit it. The off-setting debit is made against the "salary" account.[2] This transaction is shown in Figure 6.5.

It should be noted, before leaving the discussion of the general journal, that large organizations use this journal most commonly for other kinds of fund transfers. Keep in mind that we have been looking at an organization that uses only the one set of revenue and expense accounts for all of its activities. Yet, from the last chapter we know that this is simplistic. An organization may be involved in several programs and activities, all of which are budgeted and bookkept separately. For example, we looked at the Compton Opera Company that budgeted separately for its home season and its touring activities. This means that account totals must be kept separately as well. On each there will be a "salaries" account, an account for "government grants," and so forth.

Such a complex system of record keeping sometimes makes it difficult to decide to which account and/or project specific monies should be allocated when they come in or to what expense category a particular bill should be charged at the time the check is written. How much of the telephone bill should be charged to the home season, how much to the touring operation? How much of the unrestricted gift dollars should be allocated to each? Answers to these questions, made at the time the entries are entered in the cash disbursements journal and the cash receipts journal, may need to be modified somewhat later in the fiscal year.

The general journal is used to make such transfers between project/activities and/or accounts. The transfers are called "journal entries." Journal entries are especially common at the end of the fiscal year when surpluses exist in certain projects and deficits exist in others. The executive director, often with the help of an accountant and the treasurer, attempts to "zero out" as many project/activity areas as possible so that a simple overall fund balance for the organization can be calculated. The double-entry system allows this process to take place in a simple

---

[2]The effect of this debit to the salary account is to increase that account from the actual amount recorded in employee paychecks (the *net pay*) to an amount that reflects both the amount of the paychecks (as already recorded in the cash disbursements journal), plus the withholding tax amount ($331) recorded in the general journal. This total equals the *gross pay* of the employees (assuming no other deductions).

manner by using the general journal to debit and credit appropriately the accounts where transfers are to be made.

THE GENERAL LEDGER

After all the transactions have been recorded in the three journals, most of the important record keeping work has been done. Nevertheless, in order to produce usable financial statements, the information in the three journals has to be summarized and reorganized. The first reorganizing step is to add up credit and debit totals by account and summarize these totals in a book called the *general ledger*.

What is the purpose of this step? Let us imagine that you are an investor with a portfolio of stock. For each stock that you own, you keep records on the number of shares you buy, the number you sell, the number added by stock splits or by reinvested dividends. Periodically, perhaps once a month, you want to know the value of your portfolio. What you have to do for each stock is to record the number of shares owned at the beginning of the period, the number added, the number sold, and get a total for the end of the period that you can use as the basis for figuring the market value of the stock.

Now imagine that each of the accounts in your chart of accounts is like a stock in the portfolio. During a period of time, perhaps a month, there are certain additions to that account and certain subtractions. These are recorded in the three journals. At the end of the period, you want to know where each account stands; that is, you want to know the net increase or decrease in each of your accounts. This information is calculated in the *general ledger*.

The way in which the account totals are entered and calculated in the general ledger is quite straightforward. For each account, we look first in the cash receipts journal to find out whether there has been any activity during the period, and we enter the credit or debit total on the first available line on the appropriate page of the general ledger. The same search is made in the cash disbursements journal and the general journal, and the appropriate credit or debit totals are entered into the general ledger.

Figure 6.6 shows a sample page from the general ledger based on transactions made earlier in the three journals. From the cash receipts journal, the total transactions come to a debit total of $5,000. In the cash disbursements journal, the total comes to $612 in credits. In the general journal, the total for the month came to $500 in debits. Thus, there are $5,500 in debits and $612 of credits leaving a net balance of $4,888 in debits for the month. In other words, cash (for the month) has had a net increase in debits of $4,888.

FIGURE 6.6.

	CASH — CHECKING ACCOUNT						ACCT. NO. 01
DATE	EXPLANATION	FO. LIO	DEBIT		CREDIT		BALANCE
2 28	Cash Receipts Journal		5 000 —				
2 28	Cash Disbursements Journal				612 —		
2 28	General Journal		500 —				4 888 —

Has cash for the month gone up or down? Does the $4,888 debit total in the general ledger reflect an increase or a decrease in the amount of cash? Looking at the chart of accounts (Chart 6.B), we can see that "cash" is a balance sheet account. Looking at Chart 6.C, we are reminded that when a balance sheet account is debited, this increases its value. Thus, the general ledger tells us that the value of our cash has *increased* by $4,888 for the month.

Once we have finished with the cash account in this manner, we turn to a fresh page in the general ledger and repeat the procedure for the next account on the chart of accounts. Each account must be summarized in this fashion and running totals kept on a regular basis. The closing balance for one accounting period becomes the starting balance for the next (the general ledger is usually updated at least monthly). At the close of the next accounting period, the totals from the three journals will again be entered and a new balance calculated.

With the advent of the computer, the maintenance of the general ledger has become a virtually automatic process. A general ledger program automatically calculates all the balance totals at any time, simply with the press of the right button. Some programs are written in such a way that only account totals are calculated; in others, *every* transaction entered in any of the journals also appears in the general ledger, thus giving a detailed record of complete activity in each account. Nevertheless, the principal, and the use, of the general ledger remains the same in both cases, and hours of routine work are saved.

PRODUCING THE STATEMENTS—THE FINAL STEP

Once the financial information has been summarized in the general ledger, it is possible to produce the balance sheet and the income statement. There are three steps that a bookkeeper goes through prior to producing the statements.

1. List all the accounts and give the debit or credit balances for each. Add up all of the credits and all of the debits to make sure that credits and debits are in balance (that is, add up to the same number). This step is called taking the *trial balance.*
2. Make any adjustments to the accounts that may not have already been entered into the journals. Make sure that credits and debits still balance.
3. Segregate the accounts into those that go on the balance sheet and those that go on the income statement. List each set of accounts with the appropriate debit or credit balance.

Some people find it convenient to use a worksheet to help them through the steps previously listed. Figure 6.7, for example, shows a worksheet that allows the bookkeeper to reorganize information in a way that makes it easier to prepare financial statements. In the first two columns, the bookkeeper enters information from the general ledger in order to take a trial balance. Two accounts are involved: salaries and cash. Note that the credits (Cr.) column and the debits (Dr.) column sum to the same number, they are *in balance.* The second set of double columns is for the "adjustments." Because the bookkeeper did not enter the withholding taxes in the general journal until after taking the trial balance, these payables must be entered here. Notice in this second set of double columns that credits and debits are still in balance. In the third set of double columns, the debits from the first and third columns and the credits from the second and fourth columns are combined to give the "adjusted trial balance." At this point, credits and debits are still in balance.

Finally, the accounts are segregated in the last two sets of double columns into those that are balance sheet accounts and those that are income statement accounts. In the seventh and eighth columns, the debit and credit totals for the income statement accounts are carried over from the adjusted trial balance columns. In the last set of double columns, the same procedure is followed for the balance sheet accounts. But notice that now, for the first time, credits and debits are not in balance for the two sets of double columns under income statement and balance sheet.

FIGURE 6.7.

ACCOUNT TITLES	TRIAL BALANCE		ADJUSTMENTS		ADJUSTED TRIAL BALANCE		INCOME STATEMENT		BALANCE SHEET	
	DR.	CR.	DR.	CR.	DR.	CR.	DR.	CR.	DR.	CR.
Salaries		100 -		300 -		2,100 -		2,00 -		
Federal Taxes Payable			230 -		230 -				230 -	
State Taxes Payable			70 -		70 -				70 -	
Cash	100 -				100 -				100 -	
Totals	100 -	100 -	300 -	300 -	2,00 -	2,00 -	0	2,10 -	2,00 -	0

2100   2100

The Fund Balance

However, the net difference between the larger and smaller number in each set is the same—both equal $2,100. This number is the *fund balance* which, as we have already seen, is supposed to be the identical number on the balance sheet and the income statement.

Worksheets are convenient tools when financial statements are produced manually though they are not essential. The financial statements can be produced directly from the general ledger. Worksheets become completely unnecessary when financial statements are maintained on a computer. The machine is programmed to reorganize the information from the general ledger directly into a balance sheet and an income statement.

SUMMARY

There is nothing magical or mysterious about bookkeeping. It is a form of financial record keeping that is simple, straightforward, and logical. The steps involved can be tedious but they are necessary. An organization's financial transactions must be accurately recorded in the three journals. The reorganized information, at least in summary form, must be maintained in the general ledger so that the up and down movements of each individual account can be checked and the data for the financial statements made available. The double-entry bookkeeping system, while somewhat complicated and initially confusing, allows for routine transfer of information at each step along the way.

Not everyone is a bookkeeper, yet everyone who deals with financial information should understand basic accounting concepts. Trustees and staff must know how to read an income statement and a balance sheet and understand the origin of the information in them. Too many nonprofit organizations have failed because staff members were lax in the maintenance of financial records, and trustees did not bother to analyze the financial statements. No nonprofit organization can afford to be casual about its financial affairs.

7

Information
Management

The National Educational Foundation was established in 1975 as a private, nonprofit corporation to promote exemplary educational practices throughout the United States. Over its first decade, the organization enjoyed phenomenal growth. Its budget increased ten-fold and its programs and activities also expanded dramatically. One of the chief challenges of the administrative staff during that period was in the area of information management. The systems for coping with the organization's mailing lists, financial records, donor records, newsletter subscriber list, and various resource directories were all designed and redesigned several times during the decade, always with the intent of making them more efficient. This chapter describes the process by which the National Educational Foundation attempted to improve and perfect its information management during those years. The story is one of initial good fortune, subsequent reversals, and ultimate success.

The chapter is divided into two parts. The first part provides some general background on the subject of information management, introducing basic terminology and discussing the subject of computers. The second part tells the story of the National Educational Foundation. While the actual organization described does not exist, all the events recorded here have taken place. For many who have worked in nonprofit organizations, they will seem very familiar.

THE BASIC TERMINOLOGY
OF INFORMATION SYSTEMS

Few discussions of information management take place today without heavy reliance on the following terms.

— data
— information
— system

The words are so important that it is useful to define them before proceeding further.

Data is the plural form of the word *datum*, meaning a fact, a statistic, an observation. In its plural form, *data* refers to several facts or statistics that have not been organized in any particularly significant

NOTE: Many of the concepts in this chapter are developed more fully in *All In Order: Information Systems for the Arts* by Mary Van Someren Cok, with Henry Bromelkamp, Ellen Thurston, and Thomas Wolf. Readers wishing to examine sample mailing, grants management, and resource directory systems as developed for computer use will find this book interesting and helpful. It is published by the National Assembly of State Arts Agencies, 1010 Vermont Avenue, N.W., Suite 316, Washington, DC, 20036.

way. Examples of data might include: a random string of letters, numbers, or words, or an unorganized series of addresses or prices.

Information is organized data. If a random string of letters is placed in alphabetical order, it becomes information. If numbers are arranged in order of increasing size, the result is information. Words assembled to make a sentence, addresses on a rolodex, and prices in a newspaper advertisement are all examples of information.

A *system* is a related set or arrangement of things that can be used to perform a specific task. An *information system* is a related set or arrangement of information that generally has a specific function. An example of an information system is a dictionary because it is an alphabetical listing of words with associated definitions that allows a user to check spellings and look up the meanings of the words. Other examples of information systems include: an instructional manual, an application for admission to college, a timetable, a mailing list, or a W-2 form.

Much of the work of a nonprofit organization involves collecting data, organizing it into information, and systematizing that information into a form that can be used by staff, board, constituents, and the general public. In fact, the administrative staff of a nonprofit organization probably spends as much time on these tasks as on any other. Information management is such an important activity in nonprofit organizations that it is necessary to be quite scientific in approaching it. Staff members must look at information management, whether of mailing lists, bookkeeping systems, or donor records, with the following questions in mind.

- Does the system we use produce accurate information?
- Is it reliable?
- Is it fast?
- Is it cost effective?
- Does it afford sufficient security for confidential information?

THE COMPUTER AGE

Just as most discussions of information management make generous use of the words *data, information,* and *system,* most discussions of information systems today place heavy emphasis on the subject of computers. Computers often provide information faster and more reliably than any other method of information management. They have become increasingly affordable and simple to use. But the tendency to think of computers automatically and uncritically as the answer to all information management problems is a dangerous one. Computers are often the most expensive and least secure way to manage information and, when a staff is not adequately prepared and trained, they can also be slower and less accurate than other methods. It takes qualified people to take advantage of computers' remarkable speed and accuracy.

A computer is a machine for manufacturing *information* out of *data*. Put another way, a computer is a mechanized system that can provide meaningful information by sorting data, selecting from it, and performing calculations on it. Some simple examples:

> *Sorting:* a computer can place a list of donor names in alphabetical order.
> *Selecting:* it can select from that list all donors that gave over $1,000 last year.
> *Calculating:* it can add up all of the donations for the second quarter of the year and calculate what percentage this figure is of total donations for the entire year.

Of course, one does not need a machine to perform any of these simple tasks. But as organizations grow, the number of these tasks increases; they must be performed quickly and accurately, and sometimes it is even necessary to perform a combination of such tasks all at once. With the growth in the amount and complexity of information management, computers can be very helpful.

If a computer is a mechanized system for manufacturing information, how does it work? Let's compare it to another mechanized system—one used for manufacturing processed sardines. The sardine processing system requires certain types of raw materials (fish, seasonings, oil) that are put into a storage container (the can). An *input device* physically takes the raw materials and places or pours them into the can. Like the sardine canner, the computer also needs raw material, called data (which is almost always in the form of numbers and letters), and it also requires an input device. The *input device* is often something that looks like a typewriter with a television screen (called a terminal or CRT). The buttons on the keyboard allow someone to type in the data; the screen permits checking of what has been put in.

The process of input in food manufacturing demands quality raw materials. If the fish is rotten or the oils and spices are of poor quality, then the final product will not turn out well. The same is true in the "manufacturing" of information. The quality (or accuracy) of the data going in determines the quality (or reliability) of the information coming out of the machine. Computer people refer to this as the *GIGO principle*—the principle of "garbage in, garbage out." Data that is incorrect when it is input into the computer stays incorrect unless a person catches the error and corrects it.

In sardine canning, the storage container for the fish is the can.

In information processing, there are several kinds of storage containers for the raw material (the data), including magnetic tape, disks (which look like frisbees), and diskettes (also called mini floppy disks, which look like small phonograph records). The data is transferred electronically to these devices, which can store tremendous amounts of data in a very small space. The contents of this entire book are being stored on three diskettes that are kept along with seven other diskettes in a cardboard box measuring 6″ by 6″ by 1″. Indeed, one of the advantages of computers is their ability to store large quantities of information in a very compact way.

Thus far, in the information "manufacturing" process, we have seen two parts of the machine: the device for inputting data and the storage container where data is ultimately stored. But the data in its raw form, like the fish in their raw form, are of little use to us. In the sardine manufacturing process, the closed can goes to a boiler that changes the fish into its more appetizing cooked form. In the case of the data, it goes into the machine's *processor* where it also undergoes a change. The word *processor* is a very apt name for this part of the computer, which takes certain raw material and radically changes its form. Like a food processor, which can chop, grate, slice, mix, and perform a host of manipulative functions, the computer processor can sort, select, calculate, or do any combination of these tasks.

One important consideration with any processor, whether it be a food processor or a computer processor, is how much raw material it can hold. If you need to mix all the materials for a cake together and you begin loading in each ingredient one by one, you will find yourself in trouble if the processor does not have enough room for the last three ingredients. Similarly, if you want your computer to perform an operation on some data, such as arranging your mailing list in alphabetical order, and there is not enough room in the processor for the whole mailing list, you will not get the result you desire. The processor's capacity for data is often referred to as its memory size and is measured in *bytes*, thousands of bytes (*kilobytes*, or *K*), or millions of bytes (*megabytes*, or *M*). In selecting a computer, it is necessary to consider carefully how much memory will be needed to handle the organization's data.

Finally, the computer needs a device to get the "processed" information to the person requiring it. An *output device* performs this task. Here a computer system is more versatile than a sardine processing system because there are a variety of output devices possible: video monitors, dot matrix or letter quality printers, teletype machines, even amplifiers and speakers. Because sardine processing only uses one output device (a conveyor belt leading to a boxing machine), we might think of the computer as more similar to a pasta machine. The pasta machine takes in dough at one end but can produce any number of pasta products—spaghetti, linguini, vermicelli—at the other end, depending on the output device. The computer can also utilize a variety of output devices to take the information, which is stored in the form of electrical impulses, and convert it to a form—such as a printout, mailing label format, display, transmission—that a person might find useful.

The input devices, storage devices, processors, and output devices make up what in a computer system is called the *hardware*. However, hardware is of no use if the computer does not have a series of step-by-step instructions to guide each procedure within the machine. These instructions are actually a series of electrical impulses that "tell" the machine what to do. They are written, using numbers and letters, by a computer programmer in very detailed sequences and in a language that can be converted to the correct series of electrical impulses that the computer understands. These instructions are called *programs*. All the programs (or sets of instructions) that the machine uses are called *software*. It is important to remember that software occupies space in the computer's processor just as data does. Thus, when choosing a computer and attempting to determine the memory size required, the purchaser has to consider the amount of data that needs to be manipulated in the processor plus the number of bytes or kilobytes the software takes up.

There are two kinds of software—the software that runs the operating system of the computer (which usually comes with the machine) and "applications" software for a particular task that the computer is going to perform such as financial record keeping, text editing, games, graphics, and so on. The availability of appropriate "applications" software should be a primary consideration when buying a machine. There are many fine computers on the market for which very little software has been written. Because the cost of having custom software specially developed is so high, it is far preferable to purchase a machine for which lots of software has already been developed and mass produced. The availability of these "packaged programs" is a strong selling point for a computer system.

In the early days of computers, hardware was very expensive and was the primary expense consideration when buying a system. Today, the trend is going the other way. Computer hardware is becoming relatively inexpensive, but software costs in many instances are increasing as the programs become more sophisticated (or "powerful"). Many people think they are getting a wonderful bargain when they buy an inexpensive computer only to find that they have to pay many more hundreds of dollars for software before their new machine can really do anything.

Because programs are sets of instructions that allow machines to do much of the paper work that people often do, and because the actual work takes place in the computer processor, the software and processor together are sometimes referred to as the computer's *brain*. This term is an unfortunate one. Computers do not think and cannot exercise judgement. In fact, a computer is only as effective as the people who decide precisely what information they want out of the system and design the data specifications and software. Furthermore, computers are ineffective if the people entering data are not careful to input accurately or if the people using the machine do not really understand what its capabilities are and how to request the necessary information from it. (It is estimated that many computers are 75 percent to 90 percent underutilized because the people using them have only learned one or two operations and do not really know all the things the machine could be doing for them.) Keep in mind, too, that computers do break down from time to time. Unlike a staff person with a sniffle, the computer does not function well enough to answer a few questions on an emergency basis. When the computer is "down," it is totally inoperative and there is no way to extract any information from it.

TYPES OF COMPUTERS

The English language has had a difficult time keeping up with advances in technology. Consequently, there are various terms used as descriptors for kinds of computers that have no readily definable meaning. Nevertheless, the general rule of thumb goes something like this. There are three sizes of computers.

- mainframes
- minicomputers
- microcomputers

Mainframes are the largest computers and are used in the nonprofit world only by organizations with extremely heavy information requirements like universities. Mainframes are generally multi-user systems; that is, many different people can work at separate terminals on different tasks simultaneously and all of the data processing is done by the single central computer. Mainframes have a very large memory and storage capacity, which means not only that they can accommodate many users but also that they can handle very sophisticated software. Mainframes also are capable of very high processing speed.

For agencies that have complex information management problems but only require upwards of ten users, *minicomputers* may be the answer. The term *minicomputer* is a bit misleading because these machines can handle a considerable amount of data, relatively sophisticated software, and several terminals and printers. Minicomputers are used in many nonprofit agencies. They are far less expensive than mainframes but more versatile than microcomputers.

The *microcomputer* is the latest of the computers to have been successfully developed and marketed, and it has revolutionized the industry. Now for a fraction of the cost of a mainframe or a minicomputer, an individual or organization can have the benefit of many of the same features and uses that larger systems offer. Microcomputers are capable of list maintenance, bookkeeping and accounting, text editing, and various other common computer applications. Their principle disadvantage is that they have limited memory, which means that organizations with very large data needs find the microcomputer inadequate. Another disadvantage of microcomputers is that they tend to be single user systems; that is, there is only one terminal per unit. If two people want to work simultaneously, an organization needs two microcomputers. Despite these disadvantages, many small agencies have found the microcomputer to be a remarkably inexpensive solution to their needs.

Personal Computers, Professional Computers, and Word Processors   The labels *personal* and *professional* as applied to computers are more concerned with marketing than technology. Personal and professional computers are usually desk-top microcomputers that can perform a variety of functions with prepackaged software. A single personal computer can be used for playing games, for word processing, for personal financial management, and a host of other uses. Professional computers generally have prepackaged software for budgeting, bookkeeping, and other business applications. Most of these machines use diskettes for data storage. The personal computers that are exclusively home-oriented usually cannot stand the wear and tear of an office environment. Those with the label *professional* tend to be a bit more expensive but offer better keyboards, video displays, more memory, the capability for communication with other machines, and the possibility of expansion.

A *word processor* is a computer with specialized software geared toward creating, editing, and producing letters and documents. Its advantage is that it is designed to answer almost every imaginable need of a person working with text. For its size, the machine is generally quite sophisticated in the operations it can perform. Word processors often have special keys that allow the reader to rearrange the text, set up headers, set margins, search a text for a specific word (and change the word automatically if desired). Some word processors even come with electronic dictionaries. Almost all are equipped with a "list processing" function that allows for the individual typing of the same letter to a list of many different individuals. Word processors also tend to have high-quality printers that may offer several typefaces and sophisticated paper-loading options. For example, some multi-tray paper feeders allow for the first page of a two-page letter to be fed with letterhead stationery from one tray while the second page is fed with plain paper from a second tray.

There are disadvantages to word processors. Some are so specialized in their operation that they cannot do even simple calculating functions. In addition, though many are equipped with sorting programs, these are sometimes considerably slower and less efficient than programs one would find on a small computer. For people who are only going to work with text, or for people that intend to purchase a separate data (that is, numerical) processing computer, these are not serious disadvantages. In many small and medium-sized nonprofit organizations, in fact, it is word processors that have become the essential tools in information management. These organizations find that most of their needs relate to text management—correspondence, list processing, manuscript editing—and they can handle their data processing needs without a computer.

SUMMARY

The preceding sections have provided some of the necessary background for understanding information systems in general and computers in particular. They serve as an introduction to the next section of the chapter that describes information management in a particular nonprofit organization. By looking at an actual case history, that of the National Educational Foundation, it is possible to appreciate the potential successes and pitfalls in information systems design.

THE NATIONAL EDUCATIONAL FOUNDATION : A CASE HISTORY

BEGINNINGS

When the National Educational Foundation was founded in 1975, the trustees made a couple of wise decisions. The first was that during the first year of operation, the organization would arrange to have its financial records maintained by another well-respected organization in the same town. This would serve two functions: It would allow the staff more time to set up the first-year's activities without the additional burden of keeping the books, and it would also give the organization an exemplary model on which to base its bookkeeping and accounting systems during the second year.

The trustees' second wise decision was to computerize the National Educational Foundation's mailing list from the first day of operation. Even though the initial list was tiny (less than 500 names), it was thought, quite correctly, that the list would grow rapidly and that a computerized mailing list would facilitate updating, additions, corrections, selective mailings, label and list generation, and a host of other tasks. Consequently, the foundation signed a contract with a small service bureau which, for the first four years of the organization's existence, provided lists on what is called a "batch processing basis." Input was prepared on specially designed forms by a staff person at the foundation's office. Periodically, a batch of forms would be sent to the service bureau. There the data would be input to the computer, a printout would be run, and all the material would be mailed back to the foundation for checking. Whenever the foundation needed more printouts or required labels for a mailing, staff would call the service bureau and request what was needed. The service was fast enough for the foundation's needs, it was inexpensive, it was reliable, and it was accurate.

The other information system that was put in place the first year was primitive but adequate. It was a donor and subscriber file. The foundation had to maintain records on those who subscribed to its newsletter and it also had to keep records on those who contributed money. The same staff person handled both functions and her system for record-keeping was quite ingenious. She bought two metal file boxes for three-by-five index cards. On each card, she wrote pertinent information about a single individual subscriber and/or donor. In each box, she had a complete list of donor and subscriber cards. One complete list of donors and subscribers was kept in alphabetical order; the other was kept in zip code order (for bulk mailing purposes). Donors were distinguished from subscribers by the color of the plastic clips attached to the top of the cards (red for donor, blue for subscriber). Clips were attached to the left side of the card for current year subscribers and donors. At the end of the year, as people subscribed or gave money for the following year, the appropriate red or blue clip was added to the center of the card. The following year, clips were added on the right side. In this way, the staff person could quickly find subscribers who had not yet resubscribed and donors who had not yet made their contribution for the following year. The system was reliable, and initially fast enough and accurate enough to satisfy everyone; no one could complain about its cost.

During the second year, the bookkeeping system came in house.

The cooperating organization had set up a fine set of books, which a new bookkeeper simply continued to operate from. All bookkeeping was done manually—there were few transactions and this did not appear to be a burden. Financial statements were prepared by the bookkeeper throughout the year and the official year-end balance sheet and income statement were prepared by the certified public accountant who did the annual audit.

From almost every point of view, the National Educational Foundation was operating smoothly and effectively during its first four years of existence. The information systems were adequate for the organization's size and range of activity, staff and trustees felt comfortable with them, and the work was completed on time without great stress.

TROUBLE BEGINS BREWING

Ironically, the precipitating cause of trouble in information management at the National Educational Foundation was a two million dollar gift that suddenly increased the scale and scope of the organization's operation. Rejoicing, at least by the staff, was short-lived. News of the gift was carried by the press and soon it seemed as though everyone wanted to be on the foundation's mailing list. The batch processing system now seemed cumbersome and slow and the service bureau began to grumble about the rapid growth and change. There were problems in the bookkeeping area as well. The bookkeeper, who had managed quite well before the gift, now found herself working late every night. Payroll records alone were requiring an extra weekend-per-month of her time because so many new staff people had been added. One of these new staff members was a director of development (the former contributions/publications person became a full-time director of publications). From the development director's point of view, metal file boxes with three-by-five cards were not adequate for a professionally managed fundraising office. Even the director of publications, who had initiated the system, realized its limitations. Because her subscribers now were given the option of taking out a subscription in any month (formerly, subscriptions were made available only once a year), it was simply not practical to indicate subscription ending months by attaching plastic clips to three-by-five cards.

The two million dollar gift had caught the trustees and the staff by surprise. As a result, there was great haste to come up with an appropriate programmatic response to the new bounty. This consumed much of the time of senior staff and trustees. Any additional spare time was taken up by press interviews (the gift had received much publicity), long-range planning, and ongoing program management. Thus, there did not seem to be adequate time to focus on the problems of information management, and the solutions that were devised tended to be haphazardly implemented on a crash basis. The results, quite predictably, were not really long-term solutions at all and they simply compounded the problems.

The mailing list problem was the first to come to a head. The service bureau manager told the foundation's executive director that his firm could not keep up with the workload unless he was able to hire someone to do data input. He had kept his costs down, he explained, by doing all the input himself with his wife helping out occasionally when the workload got heavy. But now there was no way they could provide the level of service being requested without hiring someone and, as a consequence, doubling their rates to the foundation. The executive director, though not happy with the new terms, accepted them.

In the bookkeeping and accounting area, the executive director was faced with a second problem. The bookkeeper submitted her resignation, complaining about the workload. The executive director, somewhat desperately, asked her to reconsider. She stated that she would remain in her job if the payroll was contracted to an outside service and she was given a half-time assistant. Once again, the executive director gave in.

The next person to complain to the executive director was the new director of development. "I was told that the records were in order when I took this job," he said. "The records are on three-by-five cards with plastic clips, if you can believe it. I am going to have to hire a clerical assistant for six months to help me put the records in order." The executive director was unhappy, having just agreed to an assistant for the bookkeeper. "Can't you do the work yourself?" he asked. "Sure," answered the director of development, "if you don't want me to go out and raise any money." One week later, the development director had hired his assistant with the executive director's reluctant blessing.

Inevitably, a complaint also came from the director of publications. There was no way she could keep up with the subscriptions management and publish the newsletter. It was one or the other. Once again, the executive director agreed to an expensive solution involving more personnel. By this time, however, he knew that he had a serious problem on his hands. It was time to discuss the information management problem frankly with the trustees.

A "BARGAIN" SOLUTION

As soon as the trustees heard of the problem, everyone agreed that a computer was the solution. Discussion focussed on what kind of computer to get and how much could be saved by this or that alternative. In the midst of the discussion, someone remarked, "Isn't it true that some of the computer companies give equipment to nonprofit organizations? Shouldn't we be looking for an equipment contribution?" Everyone agreed that this might be a low-cost solution to the problem and the executive director was instructed to report back at the next meeting about the feasibility of an equipment gift.

Unfortunately, the search for free equipment took longer than anticipated. Computer companies did indeed give away equipment, but representatives of those companies suggested that the National Educational Foundation send in a "proposal." Turn-around time on the proposals took as long as seven months in some cases and the fourteen proposals that the organization submitted took up many valuable hours of the executive director's and the director of development's time.

None of the companies acted favorably on the request for free equipment. Most sent a form letter of rejection. However, in one case, a manager of corporate contributions sent a personal letter to the foundation's executive director that read in part:

"We have reviewed the material you sent us. The Contributions Committee was very impressed with the programs and activities of the National Educational Foundation. However, we are not convinced that the organization has done adequate planning for the use of a computer. We feel that a computer will not help your organization until such planning has taken place. Consequently, we do not feel we can make an equipment gift."

This letter contained the soundest advice that the National Educational Foundation had yet received in the area of information management. However, the executive director failed to take it seriously. The trustees had given him an assignment—to find free computer equipment—and he was determined to complete the assignment. His search lasted ten months during which time the information management problem at the foundation continued to deteriorate.

Finally, the search ended. An educational textbook company based in Minneapolis was modernizing its computer system. It was making its old system available to a worthy nonprofit organization in the educational field. The equipment would be given free of charge with the recipient organization only having to pay shipping costs. The executive director was ecstatic. He called Minneapolis, sent a letter describing the National Educational Foundation, and two weeks later the computer equipment was on its way.

When the equipment arrived, the trucking company required a check for $521 to cover shipping and then charged another $150 to carry the heavy machinery to the foundation's office. Once the equipment was delivered, it turned out that special wiring and grounding was required that cost an additional $250. Meanwhile, no one really knew very much about the machine and its capabilities. The executive director called Minneapolis to find out whatever he could from a representative of the company that had donated the machine. The representative who had been so pleasant about arranging the gift was now rather unpleasant: "Look, we made a gift of the equipment, but we did not throw in training. I really do not have time for this."

The next call was to a representative of the company that had manufactured the machine. "What model do you have?" the representative asked. When told, he laughed and said, "Oh, that baby. I didn't know any of those dinosaurs were still around. Do you know what programs you have? The language that machine uses is kind of obsolete. I am not sure you will be able to find many programmers around who can work with it."

Three more weeks of phone calls and the executive director realized that the National Educational Foundation had made a terrible mistake. It would be possible to use the computer, eventually. But it would hardly be worth it. At least $8,000 of programming would be involved just to design decent mailing list and bookkeeping programs to fit the needs of the organization. Furthermore, much of the equipment was so out of date that replacement parts would be a problem—the manufacturer would no longer even give a service contract on the machine. Finally, it was clear that computer technology had advanced to such an extent since the machine had been manufactured that even an inexpensive microcomputer with a few packaged programs would be a more effective solution to information management problems at the foundation than the old warhorse.

"LET'S DO IT RIGHT"

The frustration of "the great bargain approach" and other inadequate solutions led the trustees of the National Educational Foundation to try and figure out how they might develop a comprehensive, long-term, organization-wide plan for information management. Their decision was to find some professional help and, after researching the cost, the trustees committed $5,000 to bring in an outside consultant who could recommend the best course of action. Once the funds were approved, the executive director began looking for a qualified person. This turned out to be a time-consuming and somewhat frustrating process. There were plenty of individuals and firms who were in the business of *selling* computer systems. Many of them were qualified to provide advice, but the trustees agreed that these people were less likely to be objective about the range of options available. Ultimately, a young woman was selected who had worked in the data-processing departments of two large nonprofit agencies and had designed several computerized systems. At a rate of $400 per day plus expenses, she estimated that the $5,000 would purchase approximately ten days of her time, an initial information survey, and a report.

Before coming to the foundation, she sent a letter to the executive director with what she called a "homework assignment" for the staff. The letter read in part:

"The initial steps in designing a successful information system are first, to decide what you want out of your system (*determining the outputs*) and second, to figure out the data you need to put into the system to get that information out (*determining the inputs*). For the first step, you and the staff must look at each of your information areas—mail, bookkeeping, subscription list, donor files, and so on—and figure out what information you need, how often, in what form, and how quickly. For example, you may decide that from your mailing list you must be able to do selective mailings to your board (every month), your funders (four times a year), your potential donors (once a year), your grantees (whenever there is new grants information), the press (every two weeks), and your entire mailing list twice a year. Be sure to tell me the numbers of people in each of these categories, not only now but what you anticipate five years from now (we want to design a system for the future as well as the present). Also let me know whether you use a mailing house (which may require names and addresses on some special kind of mailing label) and whether you need a zip code order list, an alphabetical list, and any other special arrangement.

"The second step will be in figuring out what data you need in the system to pull this information out. Obviously, each entry on your mailing list will require at least: name, address, city, state, and zip code. (We call each of these a "*field.*") In addition to these fields, there may be others that you need such as a field for an individual's title and another for his or her company affiliation. How about a field for a descriptive code to separate the different kinds of entries on the mailing list? Do you currently have such a code that separates your press people from your grantees from your board members? By the way, as you list each field, I will need to know how many characters each will require. If the longest name on your mailing list is "L. Coe," you will only need six characters in the "name" field (punctuation and spaces between words each count as a character). But then again, you may have a Doctor Mortimer James Rothschild, Junior. If you do, I would seriously consider abbreviating "Doctor," "Junior," and possibly the first and second names. Remember, if we use a computer, the more characters we use, the larger the memory we need and the more expensive the machine will be.

"You ask how you can keep the costs of my consultancy down. I cannot stress enough how important it is for you to do a careful and thorough job before I arrive. I can do it with you, of course, but it will waste my time and your money. Please get your staff to take these tasks seriously as it will make my job very much easier."

When the consultant arrived, she spent two days going over the material that staff members had prepared. Though the preparatory work they had done was excellent, she met with each staff member individually and asked probing questions about what each had written. "You say you need to separate potential donors from those who have contributed," she said to the development director, "and that you need to distinguish between individual donors and institutional donors. Do you ever see a time when you will need to separate public sector contributors like the Office of Education from your profit-sector corporate contributors?"

During the next two days she analyzed the systems that were already in place. "If something works very well," she explained, "I will try not to change it. The payroll arrangement you have with your bank, for example, seems like a terrific deal. Even if we get you a new computer system, I doubt whether I will recommend bringing your payroll in house."

The consultant's next five days were spent at her own office completing the third and fourth steps of the job. In describing these steps to the executive director in her initial proposal she had written: "After we have determined the inputs and outputs for the system, I will do two things: First, I will *determine the best design* for your system. I will decide such issues as whether it makes more sense to centralize all your mailing lists or keep them separately in the various departments; whether you ought to redesign your accounting system; whether you need to reallocate staff responsibilities to manage information flow more efficiently. After completing that step, I will *recommend the best system* for you; best in the sense of getting a system which is fast, accurate, secure, dependable, and cost efficient. In some cases, I may recommend that you computerize part of the operation; in others, I may suggest that a people-based solution is best—for certain activities you can use volunteers and work-study students, for example; in still other cases (like payroll) I may suggest that an outside service is best. When I have completed these two steps, I will draft a report that staff and trustees can review."

Three weeks after her visit, the consultant's report was received. It outlined the consultant's recommendations. The most significant of these was that the foundation implement an in-house computer system that would consist of one minicomputer and one free-standing word processor. Initially, the minicomputer would be equipped with three terminals (with the option of adding three more later) and a communica-

tions program so that the two staff people with their own microcomputers could "bring work home" via telephone. Software options were
also outlined. Though packaged programs did exist, it appeared as
though some custom software would have to be designed. "The amount
of packaged software available depends on which hardware is ac-
quired," the report read, "and this will obviously be a factor in costing
out the best option."

The executive director and the trustees were pleased with the
report. Though they had spent $5,000 and would spend even more
before making the final decision on equipment, they at last had a professionally researched plan that would allow them to move ahead with
confidence. At the next trustees' meeting, an additional $1,000 was
approved for the consultant so that she could draft a detailed "Request
for Proposal" (RFP), a document that could be circulated to data-
processing vendors who would bid on the installation of the system. One
month later the completed RFP was received. It consisted of the following items:

- a description of the foundation and its activities
- a statement of what the information system was supposed to accomplish in broad terms
- a more specific outline of the foundation's information requirements
  (a summary of the consultant's report to the board)
- a detailed statement on the structure and content of the various sub-
  systems, including data specifications and report formats
- a parallel statement on equipment requirements, including general
  types of computers (the minicomputer and the word processor), numbers of terminals, printers, modem (for telephone hook-up), and so on
- a further description of additional technical requirements, including
  computer storage, speed of processing, types of communication lines
  (for the out-of-house microcomputers), service requirements, and future upgrading possibilities

Once the RFP was received by the foundation, it was circulated to a list of
companies and individuals that had been recommended by the consultant, by other nonprofit organizations, and by computer companies.
Fifteen individuals and firms were sent copies of the RFP, nine individuals called for more information, and four submitted bids. These were
sent to the consultant for her advice. She sent a letter giving her reasons
for recommending one of the vendors over the others. She advised that
the final contract with the vendor insist on deadlines for the completion
of work and include penalties if the work was not completed on time.
("Data-processing professionals have a hard time staying on schedule,"
she wrote).

At the end of the next month, a contract was signed for a total cost of $39,000 including the installation of all hardware and software. Because the organization did not have $39,000 available, it bought some of the equipment on a lease-purchase plan and borrowed an additional $25,000 from a local bank, working out a five-year schedule for paying back the loan. (Subsequently, the foundation received a $10,000 contribution toward the purchase of the equipment so the bank loan was reduced to $15,000 after four months.) Equipment was delivered two months after the contract was signed and software was installed and tested over the next several months.

At this point a four-month period began that the staff now refers to as "the era of living Hell." Until the new system was operating perfectly, staff members were told that they would have to operate both the old way and the new way (called *running parallel*). While testing out the new system and looking for things that were not working properly ("bugs"), they were also expected to manage their lists, mailings, bookkeeping, and correspondence in the old way. "We were supposed to do our regular full-time jobs and take on a second one," said the bookkeeper. "One day in the second month when the computer balance sheet wouldn't balance for the fourteenth time, I was beginning to think that I was going crazy. I didn't know whether to jump through the seventh floor window, cry, or quit. Fortunately, the very next time we tried the computer version, it worked!"

If running parallel was frustrating, the process of *documenting* the new system was even worse. The consultant had written:

"When your new system is delivered, you will be tempted to crack out the champagne and throw away all your old systems. Don't do that until you have written down everything you need to know about the new system: what data goes into it, how the equipment works, how to generate reports, which staff member is responsible for what task, and so forth. The system should be so well documented that if everybody on the staff left tomorrow an entire new group of people could come in and teach themselves how to operate it. Incidentally, this is also an excellent time to *train all the users* of the new system. Determine who on the staff must use the equipment and test out the documentation on them. When they get confused and have to ask you questions, revise that section of the documentation to make it clearer. If you get through these tasks, and run the old and new systems parallel for a few months, *then* you can crack out the champagne!"

One year after the data-processing consultant had sent her first report to the foundation, the new system was in, "debugged," and working smoothly. The year had not been an easy one for the staff. Two members of the staff resigned, one because the workload had become so heavy and the other because he simply did not want to work with the new equipment. Stress and flashes of temper were more obvious during the year than they had been at any time before or since. The executive director had privately wondered whether all of the upheaval was actually worth it. But in one of his lowest moments, the consultant had written to him:

"I think I know what you are going through. Hang in! Remember, it always hurts more to take a band-aid off quickly; but once it is off, the sting goes away. You will go through a lot this year but once you are up and running with the new system, you will be a very happy person. And the alternative of an inefficient operation for the next five to ten years is something I know you would never forgive yourself for."

The National Educational Foundation has been operating smoothly with its new integrated information system for the last four years. The staff has been reorganized and there are no longer part-time assistants in each area managing information as in the precomputer days. There is a centralized data-processing office, however, where much of the data input and report generation is attended to. Some changes in the system have occurred during the two-year period. New programs have been added, including one for budgeting and long-range financial planning, and one for tracking corporate contributions. In addition, because of the unusually heavy use of the computer, two terminals have been added and the processor's memory size has been increased. Finally, to correct one of the few "mistakes" in the original system, the accounting software has been redesigned to allow for tracking revenues and expenditures *both* by program activity and by source of funds. All of these changes have been easily accommodated within the framework of a well-designed system. The organization is operating more efficiently than ever and visitors come from all over the country to learn about how an effective information system works.

SUMMARY

Much of the activity of nonprofit organizations concerns itself with information management. Yet, trustees and staff rarely think of their organizations with this in mind. They tend to think seriously about the organization's mission, its programs and activities, its constituents, its funders; but information management, because it is about means rather than ends, rarely is isolated and considered in its own right. When it is thought about and discussed, it is often in connection with some other activity.

Yet, as we have seen, it is essential periodically to look critically at information management within an entire organization to see how it can be made more efficient. An outside professional can often be helpful, one who is trained in information system design. In looking at information management problems, either with or without a consultant, piecemeal approaches rarely lead to long-term solutions. Although it may be very useful to solve the problem of maintaining an efficient bookkeeping system, this will not solve the problem of mailing list maintenance or any other information problem within the organization. In the long-run, a comprehensive, organization-wide plan for information management turns out to be well worth the time, money, and effort. It will inevitably contribute to a more efficiently administered organization.

8

Fund Raising

Imagine that you are a wealthy individual opening your mail a week before Christmas. Of the 72 pieces of mail before you, there are 22 Christmas cards and the same number of requests for money. This is not an unusual day for you. In fact, during the month of December, you will be receiving over 400 letters asking you to support some charity or other. Some of these requests will go straight into the wastebasket unopened, but most will receive a cursory review. You will take the time to open the envelope and scan the contents before throwing away the material. If the letter is from one of your particularly favorite charities, an organization that you were planning to contribute to anyway, you will put the letter on a "fund" pile on your desk. In addition, if your eye happens to pick up something that makes you hesitate, you may put the letter on another pile, your "maybe" pile. What might cause this very important hesitation on your part? To quote one well-to-do woman, "As my hand is moving toward the wastebasket, I am checking to see whether there is any personalized message. Has someone hand-written a personal 'P.S.' or is the letter typed to me personally. If not, and now my hand is very close to the wastebasket, I check to see if I recognize any of the names of people on the board (this list is usually printed on the letterhead . . . or should be). Finally, and this happens very rarely, I may be struck by the kind of activity the organization is engaged in. But, to be truthful, it is the personal aspect of the request that keeps the letter out of the wastebasket. If someone has taken the time to make the request a personal one, or if one of my friends is on the board, I know I need to be a little more careful. Mind you, this doesn't mean I am going to make a contribution. It just means I will consider it."

Now imagine that you are a corporate contributions officer. This month your company will receive over 1,400 requests for money. The requests will come from colleges and universities, from hospitals, from social service agencies, from cultural organizations, and from other kinds of nonprofit organizations. You know very little about any of these fields. Your background is in corporate marketing, or sales, and you were assigned to this position with no special training or expertise. You have a staff of two people working for you. Your assistant organizes your paper work, your calendar, and tries to protect you as much as possible from people who call on the phone. Your secretary attempts to stay on top of the incoming mail, answer the phone, and type your correspondence. Both have no time to spare. Twice a year you are expected to make recommendations to the contributions committee, keeping track as you do so, of the various members' favorite charities. Your strategy, as you have often admitted to yourself, is to make order out of chaos. You advise the company to give to the obvious "blue chip" organizations—the United Way, the university teaching hospital, the orchestra—and for the balance of the giving program you try to put together a package that is consistent with the goals of the company's contributions' program. You want to get the most for the company's charitable dollar, and you want the company to look good to its customers and its employees. Just as important, you want to avoid all contributions that have any potential of becoming an embarrassment for the company.

Finally, you should imagine that you are an outside reviewer for a federal agency. Though your regular full-time job is as a top administrator for a nonprofit organization, you have been called upon to lend your expertise to the review of grant applications. Twice a year, the federal agency expects you to read proposals and then come to Washington to discuss your opinions about the material and make recommendations about funding. Three weeks before the Washington meeting, you receive a large cardboard box in the mail. You open the box to find three large black notebooks full of proposal "summaries" (there are 312 proposal summaries in the notebooks). These you are instructed to read through. In addition, you find another package which contains fifteen complete proposals together with back-up material. These you are told to "review in depth." You will be responsible for reporting on these fifteen proposals at the panel meeting. Says one such reviewer, "The first time I received a packet I wondered whether the federal agency was really aware that I had another job. I spent every night for three weeks reviewing the material. Conservatively, I would say I spent 20 hours and still did not finish. When I arrived in Washington, I found most of my fellow panel members much less prepared than I. My hunch is that some looked at the material on the airplane on their way to Washington. It was very revealing and quite shocking. To say our review of the proposals was superficial is an understatement. As a result, the predictable occurred. The key organizations in our field received most of the funding and we spent the bulk of our time fighting like cats and dogs about who would get the rest. What the experience taught me is that a great fund raiser is not someone who can raise money for an established organization—any fool can do that. It is someone who can raise money for an organization on the next rung of the funding ladder where the competition is really fierce."

The three individuals whose seats you have occupied for a moment share certain dilemmas. They know that the great majority of requests that they must review will not be funded. They all have a limited amount of time to look over the material that is sent to them. They are all aware of the political constraints that make it difficult to say "no" to certain established organizations. There is also something else that these people have in common. They are strong-minded individuals who have their own definite ideas about what should and should not be funded. Like most people who have been in the philanthropic field for some time, they have developed a technique for very quickly dividing requests into three categories: Those that should be funded no matter what; those that should not be funded no matter what; and, all the rest. In fund raising, this is called the *three-pile phenomenon.* There is a "yes" pile, a "no" pile, and a "maybe" pile; and it is the third pile which is by far the largest.

Most nonprofit organizations that are responsibly managed and provide a service to their communities are placed in this third category much of the time when they request funds. Those that are successful manage to accomplish two difficult tasks: First, they beat out the competition on a fairly regular basis among the other "maybe's"; and second, they manage to get themselves placed more and more often in the first pile—the "ought-to-fund-no-matter-what" pile. The techniques for accomplishing both of these feats is the subject of this chapter. It is essential to keep in mind that even those who have accomplished them are accustomed to failure much of the time. For the successful fund raiser, like a talented major league baseball batter, will be unsuccessful more often than successful. In baseball, a 30 percent success rate in hitting (or a .300 batting average) is considered very good. In fund raising the odds are about the same. Good fund raisers do not expect to be successful all the time. They learn that the secret of success is in improving their average every year.

PUTTING THE ORGANIZATION'S FUND RAISING HOUSE IN ORDER

Most of the work of successful fund raising comes before the point of asking for money. Potential donors must be identified. Letters and proposals must be prepared. Promotional literature must be assembled. But even before these tasks occur, the organization's fund raising house must be put in order. Some people call this "dressing up" the organization. Just as funders expect those who ask them for money to present themselves in a certain way, they have similar expectations of the organization. If these expectations are not met, the likelihood that significant funds can be raised is seriously diminished. What steps must an organization take to dress itself up properly?

1. It must put its fiscal affairs in order.
2. It must develop a convincing case for support that relates to the contributor's own funding agenda.

3. It must demonstrate a strong commitment and involvement of its board
    of directors in all phases of the fund raising effort.

FINANCES

It would seem self-evident that people should pay close attention to
financial details in an activity like fund raising, which is primarily about
the giving and receiving of money. Indeed, it is probably safe to say that
the one thing that most contributors know something about is finances.
They may not be interested in the subtleties of the organization's activities or programs but most do have considerable experience with money.
It is therefore only prudent that an organization seeking funds should
put its financial house in order before going out and asking for money.

What do the experts like to see? In general, the organization
should be able to point to the following.

— fiscal health
— financial controls
— proper financial statements

Fiscal health: While organizations should be able to show a need for
cash, this does not mean that they should show great accumulated
deficits, large outstanding loans, and an ever-growing negative fund
balance over a period of years. Chapter 5 illustrated how an organization
can show an overall surplus and still present a need for money in a
particular program or activity. Organizations with substantial reserves
and a history of positive fund balances do better with funders than those
that are constantly getting deeper into debt.

Financial controls: The subject of controls was also discussed in
Chapter 5. It is important to keep in mind that funders like to know that
their money is in safe hands. Responsibly managed organizations with
appropriate protections for their contribution dollars tend to do well
with funders. This is particularly true in cases where the funder wants to
make a restricted gift. There must be safeguards in place to make certain
that the funds will be spent for the purpose for which they were given.

Proper financial statements: To some extent, both an organization's
ability to demonstrate fiscal health and financial controls to a funder is
dependent on the quality of its financial statements. The certified audit,
containing a properly prepared income statement and balance sheet, is
an important tool in fund raising. Although it is true that donors responding to a fund-raising letter with small contributions do not generally ask to see financial statements, donors who are asked for more

substantial sums often do. If the financial viability of the organization is questionable or if there is some concern about the financial controls in place, most funders pass over the request for funds regardless of the merits of its programs and activities. To quote one wealthy individual, "I do not really understand financial statements but I always ask for them if I am planning to contribute more than five hundred dollars. I decide what I want to support and then I give the list to my accountant together with the organization's financial statements. He tells me which of the organizations look sound and which look questionable. If he expresses some concern about the financial health of an organization, I usually don't get involved."

Sensible budgets: Sophisticated funders have seen enough budgets in their time to know approximately what things cost. They have become quite expert at scanning a budget and picking up costs that look unreasonably high or low or identifying projected income that does not look realistic. Budgets that depart from the norm in this way generally cause funders great concern about the organization's ability to project the financial picture accurately. Some fund raisers make the mistake of designing budgets that project expenses at far too low a level in the hopes that contributors will be pleased that they have kept costs in line. Others, knowing the tendency of donors to give less than they are asked for, greatly inflate their budgets, hoping that the sum ultimately contributed will be what they really needed in the first place. Both approaches should be avoided. An organization's ability to present an accurate budget—a budget that is conservative in its income expectations and allows ample margin for unexpected expenses—is generally received more favorably.

THE CASE FOR SUPPORT

For nonprofit organizations, there are three steps to developing a credible case for support.

1. Identify the important problems that the organization is currently addressing or intends to address.
2. Demonstrate the organization's capability to solve these problems.
3. Match the description of the problems and the organization's approach to solving them to the funder's own philanthropic interests.

Problem statements: Nonprofit organizations are established for the purpose of solving societal problems and addressing the needs of particular constituencies. When the organizations are founded, they develop a general "Purpose" statement that lays out their respective missions and constituencies. However, this general statement of purpose is usually insufficient as a tool in developing the case for support. The board must lay out more specific goals and objectives that focus on specific problems that need addressing in the shorter term. For example, an organization may have as its stated purpose "to improve the state of medical care in the town of Compton;" but funders will want to know what specific deficiencies in the delivery of medical care the organization will be addressing in the next couple of years.

In order to be more specific about goals and objectives, it is convenient to develop short, tightly written "problem statements." For example, an arts organization in Compton might state: "In the town of Compton, two out of three graduating seniors have never heard a live musical concert." A social service organization might state: "In the past three years, requests for free meals have increased by 37 percent." Assuming that the funder agrees that the problem is a legitimate one that deserves to be addressed, the organization is in a good position to make a case for funding.

Experienced fund raisers generally agree that it is a good idea to use more than one problem statement in any request for money. If only one problem is identified, many organizations can claim to be in the best position to address the problem. The funder may think: "Yes, I agree that this is a problem, but I think that another organization is in a better position to solve it." By selecting more than one problem that can be addressed through a single contribution to a single organization, the fund raiser is minimizing the chances of competition.

Capability statements: In developing a case for support, an organization must be ready to answer an implied series of questions from the funder: "Why you? What makes your organization so special? Why shouldn't I give my money to some other organization?" The way this question is answered is through the so-called capability statements. The "big three" capability statements that every organization must be able to express clearly are as follows.

1. The program and activities of the organization are of high quality.
2. The organization provides broad service to the public.
3. The organization is well managed and has fiscal accountability.

In arguing that the programs and activities of the organization are of high quality, it is desirable to use either outsider opinions or specific quantitative indices. Arts organizations can use newspaper reviews; colleges and universities can use figures on numbers of applicants or teacher/

student ratio or percentage of faculty holding a Ph.D. degree. Organizations should be cautious about flowery self-assessments that have nothing to back them up.

Funders are also growing increasingly concerned that nonprofit organizations serve a broad public. "Service to the public" is one criterion that many institutional funders use to determine whether or not an organization is deserving of funding. If an organization serves low income people, the handicapped, senior citizens, students, and other special constituencies, that fact should be documented and stressed. Organizations should be able to point to the number of people they are serving and show a broad mix of constituent types.

Finally, capability can be argued on the basis of administrative and fiscal accountability. Although much has been said about this elsewhere in this book, keep in mind that one particularly important consideration to a funder is the cost-effectiveness of the operation. Other organizations may be able to solve the same problems and may be able to show the same program quality and service to the public. But can they provide the same level of service at the same price? If not, they are at a strategic disadvantage in fund raising. Funders, like the rest of us, like to get more for less.

Strategic fit: "In the beginning was the organization; then the board and staff of the organization had a 'good idea'; money was needed for the 'good idea' so the staff developed several problem and capability statements and incorporated them into a proposal; the proposal was photocopied and sent to 50 foundations, corporations, and wealthy individuals . . . and, unfortunately, no money was raised." Why?

Unfortunately, it is not enough to prove that an organization is deserving of money. The needs of the organization must be matched with the funder's own philanthropic interests. There are few people or organizations in the funding community that do not have their own particular reasons for giving, their special interests, their unique predilections. Organizations that are successful in garnering funds are those that take the time to learn all about donor idiosyncrasies. In the case of individuals, a simple conversation can reveal their likes and dislikes; in the case of a public agency, a review of guidelines and past grants gives a flavor of what is most likely to be favorably reviewed; corporations and foundations are generally straightforward about their approaches to charitable giving even when their procedures and policies are not written down. One fund raiser calls it "finding the donor's hot button;" another describes it as "matching two sets of needs—ours and theirs." In every case, it means developing the case for support in terms that the funder finds interesting.

It is important to add a cautionary note here. It is never a good idea to compromise the purposes or programs of an organization simply to appeal to funders. This always leads to trouble in the long-term even if it means a little extra cash in the short term. Nonprofit organizations often find themselves taking on special new programs that a funder has expressed enthusiasm for. One well-known opera company, for example, undertook a tour of the opera *Carmen* because a large national foundation was willing to contribute $150,000 to the project. The director's comment years later was interesting: "That $150,000 almost bankrupted us. We had never toured such a large production. We ended the tour with a $450,000 shortfall. I learned that a contribution can often get you further behind financially than you were before you started."

Although it is clearly not advantageous to compromise an organization's goals, objectives, and programs in order to secure funds, it may be quite possible to articulate the case for support in a manner that the funder would find appealing. Skilled fund raising requires that adequate research be done ahead of time so that requests for funds can be tailored appropriately to the predilections of the funders.

THE ROLE OF THE BOARD

The chapter on trusteeship dealt with the need for board members to contribute cash and to assist in the general fund raising effort. We have seen that funders may be very interested in the percentage of trustees contributing to an organization (the number should be 100 percent). As one funder puts it: "Trustees should always be reminded of the two 'G's'—'give' or 'get off the Board.' " Funders are also interested in the involvement of trustees in the general fund raising effort. Thus, there is a third "G"—get. Not everyone does direct solicitation; but there are other activities such as long-range planning for development efforts, research, list preparation, making appointments, writing proposals and letters, and keeping records. There are plenty of jobs for everyone. To some extent, the fiscal health of the organization depends on the extent to which the trustees feel that the income gap (the difference between what is earned and what is expended) is their responsibility. Clearly, too, board members can be extremely helpful in direct solicitation and in arranging fund raising calls for staff. Their involvement is one way that the funding community takes the measure of the organization's vitality and health.

UNRESTRICTED GIFTS AND INDIVIDUAL CONTRIBUTORS

All money raised by nonprofit organizations is not of equal value to its operation. Certain gifts are most useful because they can be used for any purpose consistent with the organization's charter (or Articles of Organization). These gifts are called unrestricted because the donor has not attached any strings to them. Other gifts, the so-called restricted ones, can only be used for a specific purpose or at a specific time or both. Restricted gifts can occasionally even hurt an organization because they require that additional money be raised to cover the cost of undertaking the project. Clearly, the most valuable money is that which is unrestricted. It can be used to pay the most basic of core administrative expenses like the rent and utility bills, staff salaries, telephone, and other office costs. For many nonprofit organizations, finding adequate unrestricted income is a constant worry. Funders always seem to want to pay for "projects" and "programs" but are less enthusiastic about making a general gift to help pay for overhead. For that reason, long-range planning in the financial area must concern itself with identifying first and foremost the sources of ongoing unrestricted support.

By far the greatest source of unrestricted income comes from individuals. Healthy nonprofit organizations generally work hard to build a relationship with individual donors that continues year after year. While each individual donation may seem small and hardly worth the effort, the total take can be very large. If a single individual gives $100 each year for ten years, and if the funds are unrestricted, this person represents an important asset to the organization. For this reason, many fund raisers tend to work on building loyalty among their individual contributors, working on increasing the number of people who give on an annual basis; they worry somewhat less about the size of individual gifts. Clearly, it is desirable to have several donors who contribute substantial sums every year—board members should figure prominently in this category—but it should be kept in mind that as individuals make larger and larger contributions, their willingness to keep these gifts unrestricted diminishes.

Individuals can be solicited in a number of ways—in person, by mail, by phone, even through the media. Whatever technique is used, the more personalized the approach, the greater likelihood of success. Some organizations have fund-raising committees that make calls on as many prospects as possible. Whether the call is part of a carefully orchestrated face-to-face meeting or simply part of a door-to-door community campaign, the success rate on person-to-person solicitation is far greater than that for generalized direct mail. Because this approach is time-consuming, the telephone offers another alternative for targeted fund raising from individuals. Schools and colleges have found great success with "telethons" in which alumni, parents, and students solicit funds from individuals who have had some kind of connection with the institution and are likely prospects for support.

Direct mail allows greater efficiency in time spent and people reached, but unless it is carefully tailored to give the impression of a personal approach, it is often unsuccessful. The "Dear Friend" fund-raising letter, printed by the thousand and sent out bulk rate in envelopes with mailing labels affixed to them, often ends up unopened in wastebaskets. Letters with stamps, hand addressed, with a personal "P.S." at the bottom written by hand, have a much greater likelihood of success. One organization that has a remarkably high rate of return on its fund-raising letter campaign makes sure that every letter that goes out has some personal message hand written at the bottom of the letter. At one board meeting each year, each trustee is handed a stack of letters and a list of people to whom a personal message must be written. Some people on the list they may know. Others they do not know. Beside each name is an indication of whether the prospect has given in the past two years and the size of the gift. Trustees are then told to write such messages as: "Your $50 meant so much to us last year. With our programs increasing, we hope you might consider a larger gift this year." Or, "As a volunteer, I have become convinced of the good work of this organization. We hope you will become part of our loyal network of supporters." The message itself is less important than the fact that someone took the time to personalize what would otherwise have been an impersonal request.

Once funds are received from individuals, be sure to acknowledge them immediately. A short personal note of thanks should be sent to every contributor together with a receipt for tax purposes: "The XYZ organization thanks John R. Moneybags for his generous gift of $100 received on July 4, 1983." Some organizations have "thank you" parties and receptions for donors who contribute over a certain sum. Others recognize their contributors in printed material such as annual reports, program booklets, and even newspaper articles. It is important to think carefully about how to say "thank you." Done properly, it can create a positive feeling on the part of the donor that will make next year's request for funds even easier.

UNRESTRICTED INCOME THROUGH EVENTS

Another way to generate unrestricted income is through fund-raising events. The advantage of events is that they allow an organization to raise additional money from people who are already making contributions. If someone buys a ticket to a dinner dance, purchases items at a silent auction, or pays to attend a benefit concert, that person generally does not spend money in this way in lieu of a general gift. Thus, a nonprofit organization can expand its unrestricted income from the same group of individuals by adding events to the more conventional fund-raising campaign.

The disadvantage of events is that they often involve a great deal of planning and work and can overtax the organization's volunteer pool. For organizations with a seemingly inexhaustible supply of volunteers (schools, for example, with a great number of parents or colleges with a large number of alumni), events may turn out to be practical. But when organizations do not have such a large supply of volunteers and have to rely either on their paid staffs or on their already overworked volunteers, events may not be a good idea.

In planning events, there are certain rules that are important to follow.

1. If the event is designed to raise money, set a dollar goal early in the planning process and stick to it. Many events planners get off course by confusing public relations functions with fund raising. The logic seems to be that if the organization does not make a lot of money, at least everyone who comes will have a good time. This has the disadvantage of taking the pressure off the planners to design an event that will reap the most money for the least cost. A dollar goal motivates people and gives them a criterion by which success can be judged.

2. Plan an event that people will enjoy. It is easier to get people to participate if the event itself is a drawing card as well as the organization sponsoring it. Avoid events that are esoteric and will not have wide appeal.

3. Allow plenty of planning time. Things always seem to take longer than expected and there should be plenty of margin for error in a time-line for a fund-raising event.

4. Build in plenty of ancillary ways to pick up money in conjunction with the event. An auction (in which people donate goods and services that are then bid on by anyone who wants to attend) can include a preauction cocktail party (with income-producing cash bar) a potluck dinner (for which people have to buy tickets), a raffle for some high-priced items, a souvenir table, a game room for youngsters, and so on.

5. Involve local merchants. While local business people may be reluctant to make a cash contribution to a nonprofit organization, many are more than willing to donate goods and services for an event. Keep in mind that even when merchants are willing to donate things "at cost" (which in fact costs them nothing), the recipient may be saving 40% to 60% off the retail price. In the same way, when the gift is made outright, it is a lot less expensive for the merchants than if they gave cash. It is also a way for them to get a little free advertising for their wares.

6. Attempt to find a type of event that works for the organization and stick to it for several years. As knowledge of the event spreads, people will begin to plan for it, building it into their calendars and their budgets. It is always best if the event can happen at a predictable time each year (like the first Saturday in February) so that people do not have to wait for an announcement to save the date.
7. Exaggerate the number of volunteers and dollars you will need in order to make the event a success. Like budgeting, planning for a fund-raising event usually requires overstating needs at the beginning of the planning process.

CORPORATE SUPPORT

The business of a profit-making corporation is to make money. When the corporation turns a profit, the shareholders are happy; when it loses money, the shareholders get restless and often fire the chief executive. It would seem foolhardy and counterproductive, given this fact, for the chief executive to recommend that the corporation give away money to charity. Yet, many corporations give away money to nonprofit organizations—some in surprisingly large amounts. There are tax advantages in doing so, but this alone does not explain why corporations are philanthropic. Usually, when corporate leadership decides to contribute to charity, the decision is seen to be very clearly in the business interest of the corporation.

Generally, one of three factors motivates a corporation to give.

1. The gift will influence public opinion about the corporation.
2. The gift will benefit employees.
3. The gift will assist in marketing a product.

Influencing public opinion: There are many companies that have generous philanthropic programs because they wish to impress the general public that they care about humanity. Oil companies, major utilities, companies that manufacture war machinery are just three kinds of companies that have a public image problem. Not surprisingly, all three also give substantial amounts to charity. In so doing, they are making a conscious business decision to invest in some positive public relations to neutralize negative public opinion. For companies that use philanthropy in this way, the more visible the project, the more likely it is to receive company support.

Employee benefits: Other companies are concerned about philanthropic programs that lead to loyalty and positive feelings among employees. Sometimes the benefits can be very direct—such as company supported day-care centers for the children of employees; sometimes they are indirect—such as gifts to major cultural organizations in a city so that employees can continue to enjoy the amenities and quality-of-life benefits of that particular locale. In recent years, corporate matching gifts programs have been popular with some companies. What better way to make an employee happy than for the company to match a contribution to his or her favorite charity?

Marketing: When a company comes out with a new product, it is sometimes advantageous to give away "free samples" as a marketing device. When the recipients of these "freebies" happens to be a nonprofit organization, the company gets credit for a charitable contribution as well. Because the company cost in manufacturing the item is usually no more than half of its retail cost, the company can magnify the impact of its contributions program by doubling what it could do with the equivalent amount of cash. At the same time, it gets its product into the marketplace and gains an advocate/salesperson in the recipient nonprofit.

Given these sorts of motivating factors, it is extremely important to find out precisely what is behind a corporation's contributions policy before a proposal is submitted. The best way to find out this information is to arrange an interview with someone on the contributions committee or the contributions staff. Here are the steps involved:

1. Do some basic research about the corporation to find out who you should talk to. At the same time, get a copy of the corporation's annual report and see whether you can get any clues about what kinds of activities were supported in the past.

2. Spend a considerable amount of time seeing whether you can find someone who will introduce you either by phone or letter to the funder. At the very least, get someone who agrees to allow you to use his or her name as an introduction.

3. If your contact has called or written on your behalf, requesting that the company representative talk to you for a few minutes, call and ask to speak to that person telling the secretary that your contact told you to call.

4. If you are introducing yourself, you can either send a letter ten days ahead saying that you will call in about a week or you can attempt to get through using your contact's name without a letter.

5. Be polite but firm with the secretary. Do not explain why you are calling or why you wish to speak to the company representative. Simply reiterate that your contact told you it was important to speak to the company representative directly.

6. If and when you finally get through, explain to the person at the other

end of the line that your contact said that he or she could be helpful to you as you plan your fund-raising efforts and that you would like to take 15 or 20 minutes to discuss your plans. If the person appears negative about your getting money from the company, explain that you really want general advice on your strategy, other contacts, and your program and that a short conversation would be very valuable in any case.

7. When you get your interview, keep several things in mind.

   a. The most important purpose of your visit is to find out as much as you can about the company's approach to contributions. The best way to find this out is to get the company representative to feel comfortable and to talk freely. Start the conversation with something informal like asking about the family photograph on the desk.

   b. The second most important mission is to get the names of other business representatives you should be talking to. Ideally, you would like this person to make other introductions for you by phone. More often than not, the best you can hope for is being able to use his or her name when you make the calls—but this is a good deal. Try to get five names before you leave.

   c. You do want to say something about your organization. Remember, though, the person you are talking to is not an expert in your field and will be bored by details. Keep your description of your organization short. Practice at home making a cogent six-minute presentation.

   d. Be sure to ask when is the best time to submit a proposal, what the usual grant levels are, and, if possible, what kind of project your organization might undertake that would most likely be funded. Do not beat around the bush. You are there to get this information and the person you are talking to expects to be asked these questions.

   e. KNOW WHEN TO LEAVE! Plan on staying no longer than 25 minutes and watch carefully to be sure the person you are talking to is not getting bored. He or she may want to keep you around but more often than not you will mistake politeness for enthusiasm. If you are unsure about whether you should continue, test the waters with a comment like, "I know you must be awfully busy and I do not want to take too much of your time." This gives the person a chance to move you out comfortably or to keep you around a little longer.

   f. Send a thank you note within a day of the visit summarizing the advice you were given. This will provide good background material when your proposal actually comes into the corporation. If you do not send a proposal within three months, keep in contact with regular letters informing the person of your activities. You have broken the ice and you must keep the contact alive.

One of the things you should find out in your conversation is the proper form for your proposal. Some corporations just want a one-page letter with a budget. Others want a more formal proposal. Unless you are specifically told to do so, do not submit anything longer than four pages double spaced. Ideally, you should have a one-page introduction that summarizes the project (preferably in bulletin-sized type) a two-page detailed description, and a budget page. Additional supporting material, such as an annual report and promotional material may also be requested.

There are times when you simply will be unable to get an appointment with someone in the corporation and this is often a sign that it is probably not worth the effort for you to send in a proposal. Organizations that submit proposals without face-to-face interviews generally do not get funded. It is true, that given the work load of contributions staff people, you may have to settle for a long telephone conversation. In certain cases, after such a conversation, or even after reading the corporation's annual report, you may feel that submitting a proposal is worth a try. You will at least get your organization's name and program in front of the contributions committee and a rejection letter may serve as an appropriate pretext to request a face-to-face meeting for a follow-up proposal. It is important to keep in mind, though, that statistics are against you and it is probably not worth spending a lot of time trying to get money from corporations where the personal contact has not been established.

Sometimes, you may discover that someone in your organization has a "contact" in the corporation who can help you with a grant. Occasionally this someone is the chief executive. Using this contact properly is extremely important. Ultimately, you want to go through the proper channels and talk to the people in corporate contributions. Trying an end run that bypasses the people who are appropriately involved in the contributions process can lead to trouble. However, it is perfectly proper to have someone in the company assisting you in getting the appointment.

Remember, in all probability, your support from a corporation will be for a restricted purpose and it will be only for a short period of time. Organizations that receive substantial unrestricted gifts from corporations on an ongoing basis are rare. This is why nonprofit organizations must assess very carefully whether it is worth spending the time and effort in approaching corporations. They must ask themselves whether they have a program that will give the company the kind of exposure or benefits it seeks, whether they have the staff resources to research and cultivate corporate relationships, and whether they want to invest so much time and effort raising money for specific short-term projects.

LOCAL BUSINESS GIVING

While the corporate community may be difficult for all but the largest nonprofit organizations to tackle, the local business community is a different story. Properly cultivated, local business should provide another source of ongoing unrestricted income. Individual contributions will probably be small, but if there are enough of them they can provide an important source of revenue. In some cases, the contributions are in forms other than cash. The local supermarket may contribute food toward a fund-raising event; a law office may contribute free legal help; the bank may contribute its advertising space in the newspaper to help promote an event. All of these contributions should be encouraged no matter in what form they come. The idea is to be as inclusive as possible in soliciting from local businesses—and the more contributors an organization has, the easier it is to get more.

In soliciting from local business, there are certain rules to follow.

1. Always have a suggested dollar range for unrestricted contributions from local business. The minimum should never be less than $50 and the maximum should not be too high (perhaps between $200 and $300). Remember, the idea is to get ongoing gifts from the same sources year after year and this is only possible if the amounts requested are modest.

2. If a new building or special project is planned, fund raising for this can be done separately and larger amounts can be requested. Such one-time requests for special items should not interfere with the regular annual campaign.

3. Make it more convenient for last year's donors to give again this year than to drop out of the annual giving campaign. You might send a letter at the beginning of your campaign asking them to let you know if they do *not* wish to be listed as a donor again this year in your program booklet. Once the booklet is printed, send them a copy, underscore the firm's name, and suggest that this would be a good time to send the check.

4. Figure out a way to thank businesses publicly. They are contributing to the organization in order to be good community citizens and they want everyone to know that they have done their part. In addition to printed acknowledgements in publicity and press materials, a "thank you" party or other gesture of gratitude is important.

5. First-time solicitation of businesses for the campaign should be done by peers. It is desirable to have a special committee, chaired by a local business person, who is responsible for this campaign. This person should find others in the business community to assist with solicitation.

6. Use service clubs like Lions and Rotary to let the business community know of the organization's activities. No one wants to contribute to an organization that is the best kept secret in town.

173

7. Do not confuse program advertisements from local businesses with contributions. An advertisement may be an important first step in winning the support of a business firm, but the ultimate goal should be to get that same business to make a contribution as well.

In general, local business support is important both for the revenue it brings in and for what it tells other funders about community support. Similarly, while funders are generally quite understanding of a non-profit organization with little support from large corporations, they look askance if there is no support from the local business community. It tells them something about the kind of profile the organization enjoys at home.

THE TEN COMMANDMENTS OF FUND RAISING

Volumes and volumes have been written on the subject of fund raising. There is so much advice that can be given, far more than can fit into this short chapter. Nevertheless, a few more tips follow. These tips, the so-called "ten commandments," represent a distillation and condensation of many ideas that, together with good old common sense, make ordinary people into skilled fund raisers.

COMMANDMENT #1—Remember, only prospectors find gold.

A good fund-raising team spends far more time assembling lists of prospects, and researching funding sources, than it does actually asking for money. Knowing who to ask is more important than knowing how to ask.

COMMANDMENT #2—Be sure that courtship precedes the proposal.

You would never dream of asking someone to marry you before you had a chance to get acquainted and find out whether you were compatible. In the same way, it is far preferable to ask for money after you have had a chance to get to know someone and to find out areas of compatibility between your organization's activities and his or her approach to philanthropy.

COMMANDMENT #3—Personalize the pitch.

Every request for money should be tailored, to the extent possible, to the predilections of the giver. Obviously, it is not always practical to customize every request. Nevertheless, every different type of small giver deserves a special approach and every prospective large donor deserves a specially tailored request that takes into consideration everything you know about his or her likes and dislikes. Blanket fund raising is rarely as successful as targeted requests.

COMMANDMENT #4—If you want bread, you need dough.

What is true for the baker is equally true for the fund raiser. Money rarely materializes without something to prime the pump. People who give money are conservative and they are more likely to contribute to an operation that already has a long list of donors associated with it. Public agencies will require matching funds; corporations may wish to see substantial earned income. But in almost all cases, donors will want to see that you have other sources of cash before they join in.

COMMANDMENT #5—When asking for money, assume consent.

Do you remember the last time someone tried to sell you life insurance? He or she never used the words "if you buy this policy . . ." but rather "when you buy this policy. . . ." He or she avoided being tentative and did not give you many opportunities to say "no" without actually being rude. A good fund raiser should use the same approach, always assuming in all communication that the prospective donor will ultimately be making a contribution.

COMMANDMENT #6—In proposal writing, if you can't scan it, can it.

Most proposals are not read carefully, they are scanned. All other things being equal, those that receive the most thorough review are the ones that are most legible and easy to read at a glance. Ample margins, plenty of headings, bulleted lists, underlinings, and other scanning devices are much appreciated. Also, of course, brevity is the greatest of all virtues.

COMMANDMENT #7—In designing budgets, use the old math.

For those lucky souls trained in the new math, they have a sophisticated understanding of mathematical concepts even though they may be a bit rusty on their multiplication tables. When asking for money, however, these individuals better get hold of a calculator and make sure their figures add up correctly. Nothing makes a poorer impression than a budget that is incorrect. It gives funders little faith in the organization's ability to handle money if the numbers do not even look right on paper.

COMMANDMENT #8—When in doubt, communicate in English.

Why is it that fund raisers think that jargon impresses? There is nothing as nice as a clear, short sentence, composed of words of one syllable or less (obviously, there is no such thing as a word of less than one syllable, but funders wish there was). Nouns and verbs, especially when they are very specific, are the meat and potatoes of a good proposal or letter. A large number of adjectives and adverbs are usually the mark of a weak request. When you claim that your organization is "wonderful," the funder is unimpressed—after all, what else are you going to say? If you want to include such value judgements, at least have the good taste to quote someone else.

COMMANDMENT #9—Don't take a "no" personally.

Fund raising is hard on people who are sensitive and do not like rejection because even good fund raisers hear the word "no" more often than they hear the word "yes." But after a time, the experienced fund raiser looks on a "no" answer to a request as a challenge—it may be "no" this year, but it will be "yes" the next time around. The good fund raiser should insert an internal translator in the brain that converts the word "no" to the words "come back." Persistence, after all, usually pays, especially in fund raising.

COMMANDMENT #10—No matter how many times you said "thank you," say it again.

The secret of fund raising is not in getting the donor's first contribution, it is in getting the second and third. Developing an ongoing group of loyal supporters is essential and can only be done if just as much attention is paid to donors after they give as before. For those contributors who give large amounts of money, there should be regular correspondence updating them on the progress of the organization's activities. For smaller donors, an occasional newsletter may be much appreciated. Mention of contributors in press materials or a special "thank you" party is another way of showing your gratitude. Never take your contributors for granted and never miss an opportunity to say "thanks."

Conclusion

Over the years, I have talked with a great number of trustees and administrators of nonprofit organizations. Many of them feel frustrated. Though they are painfully aware of shortcomings within their organizations, they cannot seem to correct them. These individuals feel helpless because they can see that things are wrong—whether with board, staff, fiscal or administrative procedures—and they cannot find the time or money to make improvements. Others I have talked to are not so much concerned with problems within their organizations as they are aware of opportunities. They realize that there are things they could be doing that would greatly expand the capabilities and productivity of the organizations they govern or manage. Often these people also feel frustrated. Because their organizations are operating so close to capacity most of the time, their staffs are commonly overworked to the point of burnout, and their budgets are often strained to the breaking point, it seems impossible to find the person hours or the money to solve problems and make changes.

Few of these individuals will ever completely solve the problems of inadequate resources, whether human or financial. Unlike their counterparts in some large profit-making corporations, few will ever be able to tackle problems through a simple reallocation of staff or dollars. What these trustees and staff members can do, however, is to take certain small steps that inevitably will lead to improvements within their organizations. These steps are

- accurately diagnosing the organization's problems and identifying areas in which there are opportunities for positive change.
- dividing these areas into functional categories similar to the categories given in the chapter headings of this book.
- further separating the problems into those that need immediate attention and those that might be dealt with later.
- developing a realistic multi-year schedule for implementing change that does not put unrealistic burdens on trustees and staff.
- continuing the process of self-diagnosis and self-improvement year after year.

This book can be used as one tool in carrying out the diagnostic process, but there are others. Consultants can be helpful in analyzing problems and suggesting solutions. An organization's own trustees and staff, given adequate time and motivation to look at things other than day-to-day operational challenges, can often provide great insight into how the organization can be improved.

But it is most important to realize that organizations cannot be changed overnight and the process of change is generally best managed on a gradual and ongoing basis. It is a truism that every nonprofit organization can do what it does more effectively. Put another way, every nonprofit organization can benefit from some change. The challenge for trustees and staff is to manage that change in such a way that its effects are positive and long lasting.

Index